GWENDOLYN MOORE
DELAINE
Family Historian

Throughout my life, I have always been passionate about family and the importance of knowing one's history and genealogy. Because of the rich history that I have uncovered about my family, I was inspired to write a book about it. Born in 1956 in Bellamy, Alabama, I am the daughter of Walter and Leola Sanders Moore and the wife of Gerard DeLaine. I have three children and am the proud grandmother of eleven grandchildren and two great-grand children. For the first four years of my education, I attended Bethel Hill School which was established by my great grandfather Tom Moore, Sr. Bethel Hill School was located in the Moore Place community now listed on the U.S. map as Moore Town in Coatopa, Alabama. I am a 1974 graduate of Livingston High School. I earned an Associate Degree in secretarial science in 1977 from the college of business at then-Livingston University, now University of West Alabama. After graduating, I was employed by the Sumter County Commissioners as a clerk in the Tax Assessors office and in 1979, was employed by the Sumter County School System as secretary to the superintendent. I was the first African American to hold both positions. After twenty six years of employment with the school system, I retired on June 30, 2005. On March 1, 2010, I was employed by Children of the Village Network, Inc. as their intervention and prevention programs director.

On January 1, 2000, I began researching and recording the Tom Moore, Sr. family history and on July 4, 2001 our family held the first Tom and Safronia Moore Family Cookout. Our family theme is "Discovering Our Roots". On July 2, 2005, the first Bethel Hill School Reunion was held. It was organized by family and friends who attended the school.

THE MOORE PLACE COMMUINITY
"REMNANT OF A TIME GONE BY"

Written History Of Tom Moore, Sr.
and
A Collection of True Life Stories

Credits
Drawings by Timothy Kent Sanders:
Air Plane, Raccoon and Hog Killing Scene
Tom Moore Family Photo courtesy of
Jesse Matthews & Thomas Moore
Author's Photo by Summer DeLaine Carter
Cover Photo courtesy of Mark Greenfield
All Other Drawings and Photos by
Gwendolyn Moore DeLaine
Edits by: Bettye R. Maye & Gwen Appleby

Written by: Gwendolyn Moore DeLaine

Copyright © 2015 Gwendolyn Moore DeLaine
All rights reserved. No part of this book may be used or reproduced by any means, graphic, electronic, or mechanical, including photocopying, recording, taping or by any information storage retrieval system without the written permission of the publisher except in the case of brief quotations embodied in critical articles and reviews

ISBN:978-0-9971760-0-1(sc)
ISBN:978-0-9971760-1-8(hc)
ISBN:978-0-9971760-2-5(e)

Cataloging-in-Publication data is available from the Library of Congress
Printed in the United States of America
Southeast Media
Gordo, Alabama

This book is written in loving memory of my parents,
Walter and Leola Sanders Moore
My Paternal Grandparents Israel and Ida Moore
My Maternal Grandparents Van and Dora Sanders
And
Especially my Great-grandparents Tom, Sr. and Safronia Beville Moore for their unselfish love and sacrifice. Thank you Papa Tom for the legacy that you created for our family.

A special thank you to my husband Gerard DeLaine and my siblings Sharon Moore Austin, Walter E. Moore, Jr. and Israel D. Moore, III for their encouragement and for allowing me to share our true life stories with family, friends and the world.
Also
Thank you to Mrs. Bettye R. Maye, Jill Samuel, Rosie R. Campbell and other friends for their support and encouragement.
Special recognition to my Aunt Selena Moore Green and cousin Willie Moore for assisting me in compiling our family's history.
I dedicate this book in the name of JESUS to my children and grandchildren.

- CONTENTS -

MY FAMILY	1
PATERNAL GRANDPARENTS	3
MATERNAL GRANDPARENTS	5
INTRODUCTION	7
ESTABLISHMENT OF THE MOORE PLACE	8
TRUE LIFE STORIES	15
(1) OUR HOUSE	17
(2) MAMA DORA'S KITCHEN	23
(3) OLD MARY	27
(4) RACISIM REALIZED	31
(5) PETA	35
(6) THE OAK TREE	39
(7) THE ROAD MACHINE MAN	45
(8) HOG KILLING TIME	49
(9) THE TOM CAT	55
(10) THE CHRISTMAS TREE HUNT	59
(11) SANTA CLAUS AND THE AIRPLANE	63
(12) THE WALKING ENCYCLOPEDIA	67
(13) GHOST IN THE CLOAK ROOM	71
(14) OLD COON UP THE TREE	77
(15) A CRY FOR HELP	83
(16) TEAM WORK	87
(17) THE UPPER CUT	91
(18) THE FUNERAL POSESSION	95
CLOSING THOUGHTS	99

MY FAMILY

Front Row Left to Right: Walter E. Moore, Jr.; Israel Donnell Moore, III; Sharon C. Moore
Second Row Left to Right: Walter E. Moore, Sr.; Gwendolyn V, Moore; Leola S. Moore

My Father Walter, Sr. (Bay): Hard working, jovial, talented and charismatic. He could dance and play the harmonica like a professional and loved telling jokes. He was always the life of the party.

My Mother Leola: Loving, kind, gentle, protective of her family and a prayer warrior. She had an unshakable faith in GOD and was the glue that held our family together. She always had a kind word for everybody and was the most unselfish person I have ever known.

My Sister Sharon (Shell): Generous, outspoken, and very dramatic with a sometime over active imagination. I have always felt that she should have gone to drama school because she is an excellent poetry writer and was very good at creative dancing.

My Brother Walter, Jr. (Jr.): Adventurous, hard working and sometime mischievous. Because of his complex nature, he often got into things that caused him to get plenty of spankings. He loved horses and fast cars with loud pipes. He would often have me assist him in putting in a motor and then we would race up and down the road listening to the pipes.

My Brother Israel (Donnie): Studious, quiet, reserved and a bookworm. He was always somewhere reading books, magazines, Archie Comics and the encyclopedia.

And then there is me (Gwen): Inquisitive, observant, compassionate and love to sing and write. I was always asking questions and watching everything and everybody. I enjoyed talking to my grandparents and elderly people because I was fascinated by their knowledge of things. I didn't understand why then, but now realize that I was absorbing and storing our family's history in order to share it with the younger generation of our family. Thank you LORD for using me as your instrument.

MY PATERNAL GRANDPARENTS

Israel Moore   Ida Mae Lewis Moore
07/13/1903 – 02/22/1992   09/19/1909 – 09/01/1994

I am so thankful and grateful to have been raised in a community with both sets of my grandparents. Our house stood approximately 200 feet from the back door of our paternal grandparents Israel and Ida Moore. Because we lived so close to them, my parents never had to worry about a babysitter. If they had to leave home, Mama Ida and Granddaddy Israel were right there to keep an eye on us. And, if for some reason my grandparents were not home, my mother would call us together and say "Your grandparents are not home and I have to leave for a while so, ya'll better not leave out of this yard. I'm leaving Gwen in charge and you better listen to her. If I come back and she tells me that one of you disobeyed my orders, you're getting a whipping." Believe me, we did exactly as we were told because we knew Leola meant business. Some of my fondest memories of Mama Ida and Granddaddy Israel's house are eating apples from the tree in their yard and drinking strawberry Nehi soda that Granddaddy gave us as a treat.

Granddaddy Israel was a big man with a hearty laugh.

He loved wearing suspenders. He was well known for making syrup, grinding corn, raising pigeons, bird hunting with his beloved bird dogs and his many fields of cotton and cucumbers.

Mama Ida was very petite, kind and soft spoken. She wore a size five shoe and her favorite color was red. I think that's why I'm partial to the color Red. She was known for her expertise in growing elephant ear plants and water Lilies. It was so pleasant to smell the fragrance from the lilies as it drifted on the wind in the afternoon. Her favorite pastime was fishing. She would sit for hours on the bank of the pond behind our house patiently waiting for the fish to bite. One of my favorite foods to eat at their house was rice pudding and macaroni and cheese.

MY MATERNAL GRANDPARENTS

Van Sanders, Sr.　　　　Dora Washington Sanders
01/22/1908 -12/28/1985　　07/14/1904-10/31/1995

The majority of my early childhood was spent at the home of my maternal grandparents, Van and Dora Sanders. During the Summer and most weekends, we were always there. In my opinion, going to their house was like going to Disney Land. Although we worked hard in the fields when there, it was also lots of fun. Granddaddy Van was our playmate and Mama Dora had to be the disciplinarian. Granddaddy had a very soft heart when it came to his grandchildren. My mother could not spank us when he was around. He would always say "Billy," (this was his nick name for my mother) "leave them chullens along, they ain't did that much of nothing."

He did special things like make each one of us our very own fishing pole so he could take us fishing on Saturdays and, he a bought us Cracker Jacks or a sugar daddy when he went to town. Christmas was his favorite holiday. He would buy a box of California Oranges, Red Delicious Apples, Brazil nuts, walnuts, Muscat raisins and orange slice candy. He would charge these items at the local mercantile store in town just so he could make Christmas special for us. Granddaddy had a special tune that he whistled. During the early years of my childhood, we live approximately 1 and 1/2 miles from them. He would walk to see us every day. Whenever we heard that tune coming through the cotton field, we would start jumping up and down and singing "Here come Granddaddy, nah, nah, nah, nah."

Mama Dora was very quiet and reserved. She loved making tea cakes and drinking coffee with her grandchildren. Her favorite pastime was quilting. She made sure that she passed this skill on to her daughters and granddaughters. Her favorite color was purple and she always wore gloves when she went to church. She was very patient with us and took pleasure in teaching my sister and I how to cook.

INTRODUCTION

A Time Gone By

As I sat in front of my television watching the news, it occurred to me that there is so much anger and confusion in the world. Gun violence is at an all time high, racism has brazenly reared its ugly head again, there are wars and rumors of wars and it's every man for him-self. "It seems," I thought to myself, "As if the concept of love among the human race has waxed cold." While pondering on these things, tears began to roll down my face and I couldn't help but wonder what in the world has happen to our society? When did we lose the ability to care for and love each other? Where did our Christian, moral and family values go? How can we say we are Christians when all we can say to the poor and elderly is stop asking for a handout. How in the world did we get to this point in America? And whatever happened to the way of life during my childhood when people looked out for each other? If memory serves me correctly is it not in the Bible that we are to love our neighbors as ourselves? Does not Acts 20:35 state that we are to help the weak? And does anyone remember the words of our Lord JESUS? how he himself said "It is more blessed to give than to receive." Didn't the first church in the Bible instruct the people to bring a tenth of their earnings to the store house? And were not those tithes distributed to the poor, the widows, orphans and the elderly?

While asking these questions over and over in my mind, I began to look back over my life. As I peered through the corridors of time, I couldn't help but smile as I thought about my over protective mother, my hard working father, my beloved grandparents, my loving but sometimes competitive siblings, all of my aunts and uncles and my many mischievous cousins. I remembered the way the people in my community all stood by each other no matter what the circumstances were and concluded that this way of life is truly "*a time gone by*". Then I thought, why not chronicle stories of the life and times of me and my family that exemplified those values while growing up in our community, **The Moore Place**.

ESTABLISHMENT OF THE MOORE PLACE:

The Moore Place is located approximately 6.69 miles from Livingston on Alabama Highway 28 East in Coatopa, Alabama. It was established by my great-grandfather Thomas (Tom) Moore, Sr. Papa Tom, as he was affectionately referred to by his family, was born December 15, 1869 somewhere in Alabama. Tom was the son of Jerry and Hellena (Helen) May Moore. Based upon the 1870 U.S. Census, Tom's parents were born in 1846 which indicates that they were slaves. Although Tom was born only four years after the abolishment of slavery and was the descendant of slave parents, he did not allow that unfortunate fact of his life to define nor shape who he would become as a man. He could easily have become mired in a perpetual state of despair by share cropping and living on someone else's land but instead, he dared to dream and was determined to acquire property of his own in order to provide a better life for himself.

Tom Moore met and eventually legally married Safronia "Mama Frony" Beville on December 28, 1897 at the home of Abner Scarbrough in Bluffport, Alabama. She was born in 1867 in Tishabee, Alabama. To this union, the following children were born: Tom, Jr.-March 3, 1889; Pearce-January 9, 1891; Lucy-June 14, 1893; Malinda- June 22, 1895; Lena-1897; Rachel December 23, 1900; Israel and Moses (twins)-July 13, 1903; Jerry-December 15, 1905 and Joseph- June, 1910. Although Papa Tom and his family lived and worked in various places as farm hands, he never gave up on his dream of becoming a land owner.

Finally, On October 20, 1905, Tom Moore, Sr. turned his determination and dream into a reality. He purchased 200 hundred acres of land for the said amount of $1,500.00. Upon purchase of the land, the property was designated as the Tom Moore Place in the deeds and became known as The Moore Place over the course of time, and recognized as Moore Town on Map Quest. On April 12, 1920, Tom Sr. purchased another 160 acres of land for $3,000 dollars. This 160 acres combined with the 200 acres previously purchased in 1905 came to a total of 360 acres.

Although Papa Tom was not formally educated, he was very industrious and an entrepreneur. Papa organized his community into a small Black Belt farm town. The layout of the community consisted of a pond, a grist mill, a syrup mill, a blacksmith shop, a small country store and a school. He placed a dug-well in the center of the community. All families used this well as their main water source. Papa also grew his own coffee. The coffee patch was located beside the store. When the plants were ready to harvest, he would dry the beans and grind his own coffee. Also, there was a community bell which was used to summon people from the cotton field during lunch time or for whatever situation that arose. On June 16, 1920, Papa entered into a two year oil and gas mineral rights lease of his property all except two acres that he set aside for the school.

    Although he had not been afforded the opportunity of obtaining a formal education, he was determined that his children, children of the community and other surrounding areas were afforded the opportunity of an education. Papa, along with other men of the community, built his school and named it **Bethel Hill**. In the beginning, teacher's wages consisted of chickens, eggs, vegetables and what little money that could be paid to them. Lodging for the teachers was provided by Papa. He provided them a room in his home. As years passed, other family members also provided lodging for the teachers. The school building no longer stands but is listed as a Historic Negro/Black school.

    Papa's home was a dog trot style log structure. The kitchen was housed in a separate building from the main living quarters. After many years of hard work, Papa eventually acquired a petal operated organ, a piano and a record player. This was quite an accomplishment for an uneducated Black man that was born only four years after slavery.

    According to my grandfather, Israel Moore, life was hard for Papa Tom and Mama Frony trying to provide for their ten children. Their days began at sunrise working in the fields and ended at sunset. Money was scarce and the clothes on their backs were patched and worn but with the help of the Lord, they were able to etch our a living. He said Papa's main objective was to take care of his family and maintain his property.

He said Papa was an humble man that never bragged, but was always very proud of his community, "**The Moore Place**". Papa Tom lived to be 72 years old. His long hard but productive life ended on March 19, 1941. He was buried at the New Prospect Baptist Church Cemetery in Bluff Port, Alabama. His wife, my great grandmother Safronia (Mama Frony) Moore lived to be 78 years old. Her life ended on September 22, 1945.

Based upon childhood conversations with my father, Walter Moore and my aunts Louise Moore Hunt, Alice Moore Brown and Selena Moore Green, it appears that after the death of Papa Tom, my grandfather Israel Moore became the family patriarch. Daddy often talked of how during his childhood he had to work in the syrup and grist mills, and how Granddaddy Israel kept the store, school, grist and syrup mills in operation. Aunt Louise and Aunt Alice talked at length of how they had to work in the many cotton, corn and ribbon cane fields. And, Aunt Selena fondly reminisced of how on Friday's Granddaddy Israel would slaughter a cow and put it in a large wooden barrel filled with vinegar until it was cured. This was called pickled beef. Then he would get a drum, fill it with fresh caught fish and fry them. He would then sell pickled beef and fish sandwiches for 25 cents at the store which, because it housed a Roc-kola, played a dual role of juke joint on Friday and Saturday nights. Proceeds from the sales were used to support the Bethel Hill School.

On designated Saturdays, people would come from miles away to grind their corn into meal at the grist mill. The customer would get the first two pecks of meal and Granddaddy would get the third peck. The syrup mill was in operation every fall from the middle of September until the last of

November. I can still see those old mules hitched to the turning pole of the syrup vat going around and around in a circle squeezing the juice from the ribbon cane. As with the corn meal, the customer would get the first two gallons of syrup and Granddaddy Israel would get the third. Just like his father Tom, Sr., Granddaddy Israel was also an industrious man. He honored his father's accomplishment by maintaining the community.

MY CHILDHOOD MOORE PLACE:

During my childhood, **The Moore Place** was a fascinating and magical community where the ills of the world had no place. Perhaps thinking my community to be magical is naive on my part, but this is truly how things appeared to me. Based upon what I see going on in the world today, I feel that the Moore Place community is a *"Remnant of A Time Gone By"*. It did and still does embody a time when the extended family played an important role in the family structure. A time when neighbors looked out for and took care of each other. A time when everyone in the community helped raise each other's children. A time when no one went hungry because, if my mother had meal to make bread for her family and our neighbor didn't, the neighbor knew she could borrow a cup of meal to make bread for her family. A time when if the garden was producing peas, corn or whatever vegetable that was in season and the neighbor's garden wasn't, then our neighbor(s) could come over and pick some for their families. A time when children could run and play outside and walk the dirt roads day or night and not worry about being kidnapped. A time when children respected their elders and obeyed their parents. A time when families prayed and ate dinner together. A time when people truly cared about each other. A time when we remembered the Sabbath day and kept it holy. A time when people had to go to their praying ground and truly seek the Lord. A time when education was important and teachers loved their students as if they were their own, and a time when everybody did an honest day's work for an honest day's pay. Morals and values like these barely exist anymore but, I'm proud to say they still do in The Moore Place community.

THE PEOPLE:

The people in my childhood Moore Place community were kind, loyal, loving, hard-working, GOD fearing Christians. Almost everyone was family. There was my father Walter Moore, my mother Leola Sanders Moore, my mother's parents, Van and Dora Sanders, who lived in the south end of the community, my father's parents, Israel and Ida Moore and my great uncle Tom Moore, Jr. and his wife Alice Glover Moore who was also my great grandmother, lived in the north end of the community. Everyone else were aunts, uncles, cousins and friends from both sides of my family. My great grandmother Alice Glover Moore was my grand-mother Ida Moore's mother. She married Ed Jones after the death of her husband Tom Moore Jr. The people in the community respected each other and their neighbors' property. The men were truly head of the household and the women were mothers to all of the community children. If a child was being mischievous and an elderly person walked up, everything immediately came to order because it was understood that Mr. or Miss So and So had the authority to spank your behind. But, in today's society spanking your own child, never mind spanking someone else's child, is deemed as child abuse.

THE ENVIRONMENT:

The houses in the community during my childhood were small wooden gun-shot style or houses with two front entrances and one back entrance. They were built from pine planks and hardwood. When the planks dried, a knot formed in the wood and then it would fall out leaving holes in the wall. The roofs of the houses were sheets of tin that had holes in them which would leak during the rain. During the early years of my childhood, there was no indoor plumbing in our homes. We drew water from the well or a natural spring. There was no indoor bathroom; therefore, we had to use the outhouse. As a matter of fact, I did not experience indoor plumbing until 1972 when my parents built our new home. The homes in our community were heated by old pot bellied wood burning heaters or fire places and we cooked our food on wood burning stoves. The grist mill, syrup mill, small country store and the two room school established by Papa Tom were still in operation. I actually attended the school until I reached the fifth grade.

There was a pecan orchard, wild plum groves, black berry thickets and a variety of fruit trees. There were fields of corn, cotton, cucumbers, sweet potatoes, ribbon and sorghum cane and peanuts. There were fishing ponds, mules, horses, cows, chickens, turkeys, hogs, goats, ducks, geese and guineas. Because we lived on the farm, we basically raised everything we ate. Our parents only went to town to buy items such as flour, sugar, salt, black pepper, vinegar, baking powder, baking soda and vanilla flavor. We had to pick cotton, pull corn, pick cucumbers, dig sweet potatoes, pull peanuts, strip cane, milk the cows, feed the hogs and put up the chickens. My mother and grandmothers canned fruits and vegetables at home. Store bought foods were a rarity in our home and oranges and apples were not seen until Christmas. We worked hard but, we were happy. Our community was rural and isolated but we were never lonely. We traveled on dirt roads because there was no pavement or asphalt except the main highway. Although we were not rich financially nor did we have a lot of material things, we were rich in love, respect and community togetherness.

TRUE LIFE STORIES:

"*Remnant of A Time Gone By*" consists of a collection of true life stories and incidents that span from 1953, the turbulent 1960's civil rights movement, the 1970's, 1980's and other years that happened in my family and community during my childhood. In these stories, you will experience through my eyes the everyday hustle and bustle of our lives, the struggles we endured, the holidays we shared, the food we ate, the school we attended, the houses we lived in, the churches we attended and the love we shared in the Moore Place community. These stories are filled with laughter, love, faith, childish mischief, life lessons, ghost stories and even a little bit of sadness. It is my desire that the recording of these true life experiences will serve as a reminder of a bygone time that can be used by future generations that would like a glimpse into the past.

OUR HOUSE

Sometime during the year of 1953, my father built a little three room L shaped house with a front porch for his new bride, Leola Sanders. For the first 14 years of my life this little house was home to my parents and their four children. It was crudely constructed from lumber that was given to my father by an elderly white couple as payment for tearing down their old house. The lumber was a mixture of hardwood and pine. The pine lumber was used to build the walls of the house. Pine planks are prone to form knots in them when they become dry which caused a problem because the knots would fall out leaving holes in the walls. There was no insulation; however, during the summer months, the holes served as an air conditioner to help keep the house cool. This was not true during the winter. On those cold winter days, my mother would take old rags or socks and stuff in the holes to keep the cold air out.

The windows were very fragile and in the winter the wind seemed to penetrate through them. My mother and grandmother would nail quilts over the windows in order to combat the cold. In later years an additional layer of ply-pane plastic was nailed to the windows as well as the quilts to help reduce the amount of cold air that was seeping in around them. Often times, while lying in bed at night, my sister and I would laugh and say, "Seems like there are as many quilts nailed over the windows as there are on our bed."

The roof of our little house was made of tin. Each sheet of tin was nailed to the rafters. The nails in the tin caused holes to form in the roof. On rainy days, it seemed that every bucket, pot and pan that my parents owned was placed on the floors to catch the rain. The only place in the house that did not leak was the right corner of my parent's bed room. The furniture we owned was a dresser, vanity, chifforobe and two cane bottom chairs. During the rainy days, these items were placed in the corner by my parent's bed so they wouldn't get wet. Because of these holes, we could actually lie in our bed and see the stars.

The floors of the house were hewn from some type of crude hard wood planks that had ridges in it. There were spaces between the planks therefore; they were covered by a thin piece of army green looking linoleum to keep us from getting splinters in our feet.

The first room of the house had dual functions. It served as my parent's bedroom and also as the living room. It was furnished with an old wrought iron bed, a chair, the vanity and a pot bellied wood burning heater. Over the head of their bed was the electrical breaker box and connected to that box were old heavy duty gray/black electrical wires that ran along the rafters in the roof of our house. The wires were exposed and could have been very dangerous to us, but we knew not to touch them.

The second room served as the bedroom for the children. It was furnished with a wrought iron bed, a wood burning heater, the dresser and the chifforobe. The miracle in this is that all of the furniture was able to fit in that one small room. The vanity, dresser and chifforobe was the first set of furniture my father bought for our mother. It was her wedding gift. The dresser and vanity set was made out of black walnut wood with brass hardware and the chifforobe was made out of pine that had been painted brown. This furniture still remains in our family.

    Our father decided not to build our modest little home in the traditional shotgun shape. Instead, he attached the kitchen to the left side of the second room thus making it an L shaped structure. The kitchen was furnished with a homemade wooden table, two wooden chairs, a wood burning stove and an International Harvester deep freezer. Also, there was a little wooden pantry built on the right side of the stove and a little wooden stool that my father built for us to stand on. There was a set of three steps that led out of the back door of the kitchen. There was no indoor plumbing which meant we had to carry water from the community well. During the day we would use an outhouse as our toilet and a slop jar at night.

    As the years passed and my two brothers got older, my father added a room to the left side of the front room. The new addition turned the house into a square shape. This room was furnished with a brown faux leather sleeper sofa thus, providing sleeping quarters for the boys. Our father then attached a wood rail onto the front porch of the structure. A #10 zinc tub with a tin and wood rub board for washing clothes was placed on the porch. In later years the tub and rub board was replaced with an old wringer type washing machine.

    Our house was located in the middle of a field. At one time or another it was usually surround by cotton or corn. In order to break up the monotony of the fields, my mother created a beautiful flower garden on either side of our front yard.

On the left side of the yard was an apricot tree that was surrounded by petunias, purple verbenas and a beautiful pink rose bush which was my mother's pride and joy. On the right side of the yard was a peach tree that was surrounded by a variety of lilies and old maids. On the left side of the house was a holly hock tree that had beautiful red and white blossoms. On the right side of the house stood a large persimmon tree which provided plenty of shade during the summer. I spent many hours sitting under that tree making mud cakes, day dreaming and reading books.

Situated in the back of the house was a smoke house, an outhouse and a fishing pond. A wire fence was placed between our home and the pond to keep the children from falling into the pond. I really loved our little home and often wonder how in the world we all fitted in that little place. As a child, it never dawned on me that the space was so limited. All I know is there were many special holidays, some sadness and tears and lots of laughter.

Also, our little house was the social hub of the community. For it was there that every girl came to get her hair pressed with an old fashioned hot comb and ears pierced with a burned sewing needle and black thread. It was there that the ladies mission would hold their meetings on Sunday afternoons. It was there family members gathered on weekends to watch Wagon Train, Alfred Hitchcock and The Twilight Zone on an old black and white RCA Victor Television. It was there that all our family and friends came to get cake or sweet potato pie when they came to visit for the holidays from up north. It was there that all the children would gather and play hop scotch or ring games. Furthermore, it was there where everyone congregated to mourn the dreadful news of the assassination of Dr. Martin Luther, King, Jr. But of all these things, the most cherished memories of my childhood in that little house are the hugs and kisses that we received from our mother as she tucked us in bed each night. I can still feel her warm embrace and the tenderness of her kisses as she said "Good night babies, Mama loves you."

Our house may have been small but the love that we received while living there had no boundaries. Although it is dilapidated, our humble little home still stands.

MAMA DORA'S KITCHEN

Sometimes while sitting around the kitchen table sharing childhood memories with my grandchildren, the vision of sitting around the old homemade wooden table drinking coffee in my Grandma Dora's kitchen is revived. The beautiful memory of those precious moments still brings a smile to my face. I can still see that old bent up coffee pot sitting on top of her wood burning stove that always had a bounty of biscuits or tea cakes in the warmer. I can still smell the heavenly aroma of the coffee as we watched the fascinating sight of the beautiful brown nectar bubbling up and down in the glass percolator. And, I can still hear that gurgling noise as we anxiously awaited for it to finishing brewing. Mama Dora would give each one of us a saucer and coffee cup. She would pour water in the cup, add enough coffee to make it brown and sugar to make it sweet. Once our coffee was prepared, she would then pour herself a cup, take a seat and say "So what do my babies want to talk about today?"

How clever of her. By doing this, she had created a loving and joyful environment that made us feel comfortable enough to tell her whatever was going on in our lives. This was one of her many ways of bonding with us, finding out exactly what we were thinking while simultaneously making sure that everything was ok with her grandchildren. Although I didn't realize it then, I now understand the important role of an extended family. She also used this time as teaching moments. It was during these coffee sessions that life lessons such as respecting your elders, obeying your parents, working for a living, the importance of getting an education, how to show love to each other and the importance of having GOD in our lives were taught. It was in her kitchen where she shared her wealth of knowledge and experience with us.

She would talk to us about the hardships of her childhood, how her mother died when she was a child and how she and her siblings were passed from one relative to the other. But, she declared, in spite of all the tragedies in her life, she refused to let them keep her down. And she said, "You, my children must never let hard times hold you back nor keep you down."

"Yes ma'am," we replied, as we poured our lukewarm coffee into the saucer and drank it with glee. As children, we didn't fully understand all that she was talking about but, we knew whatever she was saying had to be right so we just nodded our heads in agreement.

It was also in this kitchen on that old four eyed wood burning stove that I had my very first cooking lesson. Mama, as I called her, was very patient with me. As far back as I can remember, she would place me in a chair in the kitchen so I could watch her cook. "Please Mama, please let me make the corn bread?" I would always ask. "I know what to do because I watch you all the time."

"You're too small, Candy Doll," said my grandmother. "Mama don't want you to get burned. But, I promise, I'll let you cook when you get a little older." Finally, one day when I was about six years old, she gave in and said, "Today you make your corn bread." Those words were like music to my ears. How happy I was, because I was finally going to cook with my grandma.

Because of my short height, Mama had to pick me up and let me stand in a chair at the table. She tied an apron around my waist, placed a mixing bowl and all of the necessary ingredients on the table, handed me a big wooden spoon and said "Make your corn bread."

Clapping my hands with excitement, I poured all of my ingredients in the bowl and started stirring. What a sight, corn meal and flour flew everywhere. It was like a dust storm in that kitchen but, my patient grandmother only smiled and said "You're doing a good job baby, just keep stirring." Satisfied that all of my ingredients were completely mixed, I proudly announced that my bread was ready to go into the oven. Mama looked at the batter, poured it into a cast iron skillet, placed it in the oven and said, "This is going to be some good corn bread." After what seemed like forever, the corn bread finally finished baking. Mama took it from the oven and placed it on the table. Granddaddy Van, who had just entered the kitchen, exclaimed that something sure smelled good.

"What you cooking Dora?" he asked. Looking at me as I proudly stood beside the table, Mama said, "Candy Doll just made her first pan of corn bread especially for you." Handing him a butter knife, she said, "Cut a piece and see how it taste."

Granddaddy looked at the bread which was hard, flat and cracked on the top and said "Why do I have to be the guinea pig?"

"Van," said my grandmother with a scowl on her face, "don't discourage the child; just eat the bread." Not wanting to hurt my feelings, Granddaddy sighed, cut a small piece of bread and ate it.

"How does it taste?" I asked with a big grin on my face.

"It was just right Grandbaby, just right." After that first lesson, there were many more cooking adventures that took place in Mama Dora's kitchen. And, my poor Granddaddy Van was always the guinea pig.

I will always remember that old bent up coffee pot, the black cast iron skillets, the jars of home canned fruits and vegetables and the endless strings of dried red pepper that hung by the kitchen door. But most of all, I will forever cherish the love, patience and encouragement that I received in Mama Dora's Kitchen.

OLD MARY

Old Mary was a hateful old mule that was owned by my great grandmother Alice Jones, affectionately referred to as "Mama Alice" by her grandchildren. As a little girl, I often saw Old Mary running baby calves around and around in the pasture. She would literally run them until they collapsed. As a matter of fact, that old mule would run anything, "with the exception of Mama Alice", that stepped into the pasture, especially the children.

Mama Alice was a stern but very sweet lady. She was small in stature, had a sharp tongue and had no problem with, as she called it, putting you in your place. She did not mince words. What came up, came out. You never had to guess what she was thinking. Mama Alice was a great gardener. And, in my opinion she was a natural born horticulturist. She grew all kinds of vegetables and fruit trees but, was very well known for her peach orchard. She would often have us children come to her house to work in the orchard. To keep the peach trees healthy, she would cut green sapling switches and instruct us to whip the bark all around the trunk and then she would take ashes from the fireplace and sprinkle it around the root of the trees. According to her, whipping the trees made them thrive and the ashes kept the peaches worm free. Whether or not this method was true or not, I don't know but, apparently she was right because she had the best peaches for miles around.

In order to get to Mama Alice's house to perform our duties, we had to go through the very pasture in which Old

Mary resided. Oh my, what a feat that was. It was like running a marathon on a daily basis. The routine was, one child would serve as the look out to see if Mary was in sight and every time that old mule was nowhere to be seen. But, without fail, as soon as it was determined that the coast was clear and the rest of us climbed over or under the fence into the pasture, Old Mary would appear. She would come charging out of the blue with her ears laid back and her gums exposed trying to bite you. Lickety-split like jack rabbits, we would take off running, crying and screaming trying to make it to Mama Alice. This scene played out every day until one hot summer day in August of 1967 during Revival time, when all of the running came to an end for me.

In the area of Sumter County where I lived, Revival season usually ran from the first week of August through the last week of September. During this time, there was no playing, no watching television, no listening to the radio and certainly no dancing. You had to go to your praying ground during the day until it was time to go to church for Revival Services or "Track Meeting" as it was sometimes called.

At my home church, which was Christian Valley Baptist, the service was a two week affair. The first week was prayer service and the second week was preaching. It was during the first week that I had been on the mourner's bench praying and seeking JESUS. Finally on that Friday, I made up my mind and went into an earnest and sincere prayer for salvation. At the end of the prayer, I asked GOD to let me feel his Holy Spirit if he was truly going to save my soul. As soon as I finished praying, the LORD granted my request. The Holy Spirit showered down upon me and I started running to find my mother to share the good news with her.

During my childhood days, it was customary that you go from house to house sharing your testimony of salvation. Well, one of the first persons that I wanted to share my news with was Mama Alice. "Oh my," I thought to myself, "I'm going to have to run from Old Mary." As I approached the fence, Mary was nowhere in sight. But just as soon as I climbed over the fence, Mary appeared from a dense grove of trees and started running toward me. My first instinct was to turn and run back home but, something within me would not let me do so. I was determined to share my testimony. It was at this juncture that I decided no more running! As Mary came charging toward me, I held my right hand out in front of me and exclaimed in a loud and commanding voice, "Stop in the name of JESUS!" And just like that, Old Mary came to an abrupt and complete stop.

For what seemed like an eternity, we both just stood and stared directly into the other's eyes. Finally, I spoke and said, "Mary, not today. I will not run from you today nor will I ever run from you again." As if understanding the words I had just spoken, Old Mary dropped her head and looked down at the ground. I then dropped my hand and started walking right passed that old mule. It seemed as if I was walking in slow motion but, I finally made it to the gate that led to Mama Alice's house. Upon entering the gate, I looked back and saw Old Mary walk out of sight back into the grove of trees where she would hide out. From that day forward, I never had to run from her again. Whenever I stepped into the pasture, Old Mary would come out of the grove, look at me, then turn and walk away. She repeated this pattern with me until the day she died.

To this day, I have always believed that Mary stopped running after me because she recognized the Holy Spirit that was upon me.

RACISIM REALIZED

In my opinion, my mother was our biggest cheerleader. There was nothing she would not do for her children. Why, I believed she would have fought a grizzly bear with her bare hands in order to defend us.

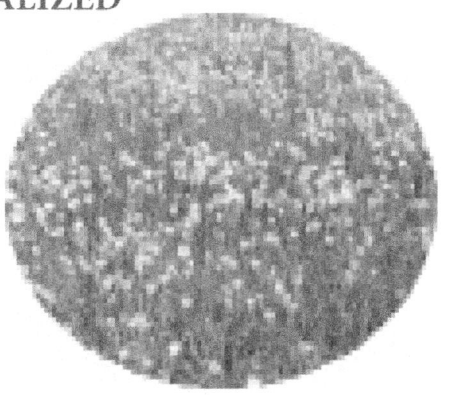

There have been many days when my mother would go hungry because there was not enough food for everyone. On those days, she would prepare our plates, let us eat first and whatever was left, she would eat. Because we were aware of what our mother was doing, my sister and I would purposely leave some of our food so she could eat. Sometimes, our meals consisted of only home-canned peaches from the jar, and biscuits. On a good day, we would each have a piece of chicken. My brothers had a drumstick each, my sister and I got a wing each, my father got the back and the breast and my mother would eat the neck. The thighs were saved to make chicken and dumplings for the next day. There were no seconds on the meat. Because of her unselfish sacrifice, I was always trying to find a way to cheer her up.

Wildflowers were plentiful where we lived. Therefore, they were the only thing I could give her that did not require money. Looking up at my mother with a big grin on my face, I would hand the flowers to her and say this is for you Ma-dear. Although my mother had a severe hay fever problem and the flowers would throw her into a sneezing frenzy, she always received the hodgepodge bouquet with a big smile and hug. "Thank you baby, I just love them" was always her reply. After receiving my hug, I would run off to play while feeling happy that I had made my mother smile. But sadly, today would not be one with the all too familiar happy ending. No, today would be one of sadness and the realization of the awful hate that existed in the world.

After finishing my evening chores of feeding the chickens, I picked up the jar of wildflowers I had gathered earlier in the day for my mother. I was so happy and proud of the beautiful bouquet and couldn't wait to see the smile on her face when I gave them to her. As I ran into the house with flowers in hand, the vision of her smile that was formed in my mind was quickly shattered.

My mother was crying and screaming, "Lord, have mercy! Lord, have mercy! What are the poor and Black people going to do now?" Although I had often heard her cry at night because of the everyday struggles of life, this cry was different. It was filled with hopelessness, despair and total defeat. Startled by the dismal look of sadness on her face, I dropped the flowers and ran to my mother screaming, "Ma-dear, Ma-dear, what's wrong? Are you sick? Are you hurting?" I didn't know what to think. Rendered speechless by the shock of the unexpected tragedy that had taken place, she could only point to the television.

Eventually, my mother was able to speak. Still crying and shaking her head in disbelief, she asked, "Why is it that anyone trying to make life fair for Black and poor people is killed? Are we not human beings bleeding red blood just like everyone else?" Still not understanding and desperate to make sense of the situation, I turned to the television to see what was going on. And there it was. The news reporter was announcing that Dr. Martin Luther King, Jr. had been assassinated.

As the news began to spread, other family members in the community started coming to our house. Everyone was in tears and the only thing they could do was hug each other and ask the question why? With tears streaming from her eyes, my grandmother Ida turned to my mother and said ,"They've already killed President Kennedy now Dr. King." What a sad day it was in my home, in our community and in the entire world.

Although I was a young child of eleven years old, the memory of that day will be forever etched in my mind. All night long I wondered to myself, why in the world are we Black people hated so much? I simply could not understand it. I guess because my parents taught us that GOD made all people equal and never to hate or mistreat anyone, it just didn't register with me that people could be so mean. What a sad, sad time it was for me. April 4, 1968, the date that I realized racism.

As I look back over the years, I realize what a struggle it was for my people during the Civil Rights Era. I often talk to my grandchildren about the sacrifices that were made in order for African Americans to obtain the right to vote. And, I think about the march from Selma to Montgomery, the bombing of African American churches, the loss of innocent lives, dogs being released on human beings during peaceful demonstrations, separate public facilities, inadequate schools and housing, limited access to gainful employment and blatant discrimination everywhere. All of this hate, anger and racial injustice because we as a people sought our basic human rights. But through it all, GOD sustained us and he gave us a man, by the name of Martin Luther King, Jr., who had a dream of freedom and equal rights for all people.

PETA

Organic farming is all the rage now. But, as far back as I can remember, my grandparents have always farmed organically. The only fertilizer we used in our garden was a cow and chicken manure mixture. Granddaddy Van said the acidity of the chicken manure was so strong until using it alone would burn the seeds. Whether this was true or not, I don't know. But, we sure had beautiful and healthy vegetables every year.

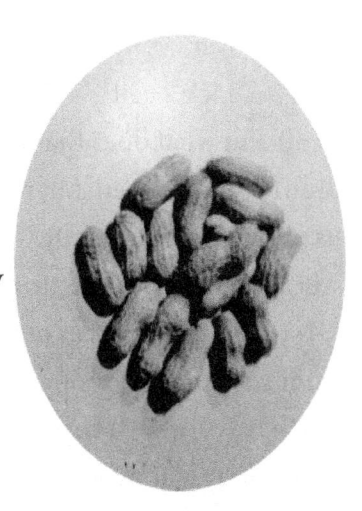

Granddaddy Van was a passionate, skilled and accomplished farmer. He knew exactly when to plant what crop because, he always consulted the *"Farmer's Almanac"* and studied the status of the moon. There were certain vegetables planted on the new moon, the half moon or the full moon. Every aspect of planting was precise and he never wavered from his routine. For example, if we were planting peas in the garden, every hole had to be so many inches apart and only three peas per hole was allowed. He made sure of the count because as we dropped the peas in the hole, he came behind us with a hoe covering them with dirt. If the count was not exact, he would say, "Y'all little hard headed rascals. Didn't I tell you three peas in each hole?"

Snickering and looking at each other, we would all reply "Yes sir," in unison.

"Well," he would say, "come right on back and do like I told you. If you do right the first time, you wouldn't have to lick the calf over."

"Lick a calf?" I thought to myself. "Who wants to lick a calf and what does that have to do with dropping peas?" I didn't realize it then, but now I understand that he was teaching us to do things correctly in the beginning so you never have to worry about repeating that task again.

Another aspect of organic farming was to save seeds from your current crop to be used for next year's planting. There was always a barrel set aside to store seed for the next year. Granddaddy was very adamant about us not touching the seeds he had set aside. He was especially particular about his seed peanuts. "Peta," he would say, "I'm putting you in charge of my peanut barrel. If anybody touch it you let me know." My grandfather has always called me Peta.

Out of curiosity, I finally asked him, "Why do you call me Peta?" Well, this is the story behind that name.

When I was about four years old, Granddaddy had gone to town to take care of some business. While he was away, Mama Dora, my mother and Aunt Mamie took some of his seed peanuts from the barrel and cooked them. They shared the peanuts with me and instructed me not to tell Granddaddy. Upon his return from town, I ran to Granddaddy so he could pick me up. "What did you bring me?" I asked.

With a mischievous twinkle in his eyes, Granddaddy said, "You little begging thing, what make you think I bought you something?"

With a big grin on my face I replied, "Because, you always bring me something." After a brief hug, and a poke on my cheek with his prickly beard, Granddaddy reached in his pocket and gave me a piece of peppermint.

Poking us on the cheek with his beard was his way of showing affection to his grandchildren. He would always say "Come here and let Granddaddy stick you with his beard." We happily complied with his request because we knew this meant he loved us.

As the day went on, Granddaddy noticed that I kept asking Mama Dora and my aunt for some Peta. Trying to play it off, my aunt took me by the hand and said go play with the other children.

"What is that baby talking about asked Granddaddy?" "I don't know," said my mother.

Finally, my grandfather decided to get to the bottom of the mystery. Taking me by the hand Granddaddy asked "What does Granddaddy's baby want?"

"Peta," I said pointing toward the crib house.

With a puzzled look on his face, Granddaddy turned to my mother and asked, "What in the world is a Peta?"

Trying not to give herself away, my mother quickly replied, "I don't know."

"I tell you what," said Granddaddy, "show me what you talking about child." According to him, I took his hand, went straight to the seed peanut barrel and said "Peta". It was at this point that my grandfather realized I was asking for a peanut.

"Well, well, well," said Granddaddy, "So that's what you were asking for." Picking me up, Granddaddy went to my grandmother and said "Didn't, I ask y'all not to touch my seed peanuts? I left peanuts still on the vine in the crib house for y'all".

"Awe Van," said Mama Dora calmly, "We didn't get but a few. Besides, I didn't feel like picking them off the vine and you certainly have more than enough for next year." Realizing that they had been busted, my mother and aunt apologized to my grandfather and vowed never to touch his seed peanuts again.

From that day until his death, Granddaddy Van called me Peta. He never called me by my proper name.

THE OAK TREE

During each person's life time, there is one thing or object that seems to be an ever present fixture. For me, that one object would be the grand old oak tree that stands in my grandparent's Van and Dora's yard. The oak was there when my mother was a child, when I was a child and when my daughter, Summer was a child. The oak has served in many capacities. It has been shade for the family when the sun was beaming down; It has been a place to hide behind when we played five, ten, fifteen twenty (aka hide and go seek); It has been the tent to place your cotton under during cotton picking time; It has been a pavilion for our many family gatherings; It has provided an endless supply of switches for Mama Dora to use when chastising her children and grandchildren; Also, it has provided a bounty of nuts for the squirrels and shelter for the many birds to build their nests. The old oak tree had a hollow in it which we children would climb up in to hide from our grandmother or to pretend that we were ship wrecked and this was our only place of shelter. It had big large roots that ran on top of the ground like veins on the top of one's hand. And, when our imagination was really running wild, we would pretend it was a monster from outer space disguised as a tree and the roots were long fingers trying to grab our ankles and trip us up.

One incident that occurred in connection with the oak tree involved a snake. As it happened, one hot July day, Granddaddy Van had just come in from plowing his mules Old Jig and Old Charlie.

"Peta.," said my grandfather to me. "Go in the kitchen and bring me a glass of water. It's hot as a fox out in that field today."

"Yes sir," I said. Granddaddy had just finished plowing a twenty acre field of cotton and had stopped to take a break before starting on the other twenty acres. As I ran up the steps into the house to get the water, I noticed my brother Jr. and several other boys shooting marbles in the dirt under the oak tree. I wanted to join in the game so, I hurried into the kitchen to fetch the water. "Here you go Granddaddy," I said, handing him the glass of water.

"Thanks Peta," he said, "That sure hit the spot." After finishing his water, Granddaddy laid down on the porch floor. "I'm going to take a quick nap so, don't y'all get in no trouble."

"We won't," I said.

My brother Jr. and the boys were still shooting marbles when suddenly one boy looked up and said, "I see a snake up in the fork of the tree."

"Where?" I asked, looking up in the tree. "I don't see a snake."

"Look right there, he just moved".

"Where, where?" I asked jumping up and down.

"Right there," said my brother.

The boys started throwing sticks up in the tree. One of the sticks hit the snake and down it fell, right in the middle of us. It was a big long chicken snake. Everyone fell backwards except my brother Jr. He immediately picked up a stick, hit the snake and knocked it unconscious. "Ok scaredy cats," he said, "y'all can get up now".

"Whew!!" exclaimed one of the boys. "That was close."

Looking down at the snake as it lay motionless on the ground, my brother said, "Bet you it ain't dead; and I can prove it."

"How?" asked one of the boys.

"Well," said my brother, "snakes can't stand gasoline so, if I pour some on it and it doesn't move then it's dead. But, if he's still alive, then it will take off running."

"I didn't know snakes could run," said Donnie, with a crooked smile on his face.

At that point, Jr. went behind the house, got some gasoline from the smoke house and threw it on the snake. As soon as the gas hit the snake, it took off crawling as fast as it could out through the field of green cotton.

"Look out y'all!" exclaimed my brother Jr. "I told you he wasn't dead. Just look how fast that thing can crawl".

All of the boys started yelling and running behind the snake. They made such a commotion until it startled my grandfather from his nap. He jumped straight up and yelled, "What in the world is going on?"

"Look," I said pointing toward the field. All you could see was the snake crawling as fast as it could with the boys right behind it. Well that didn't set too well with my grandfather because, they were messing up his newly plowed rows.

"Hey!" he said, "I know so well y'all little hard headed rascals ain't running through my cotton trampling it down. I know y'all better get back here right now." Immediately, all of the boys stopped in their tracks, turned and came running back to the house. "Didn't I tell y'all not to get in trouble?" said my grandfather.

"Yes sir," they all replied, "but, we didn't do anything wrong. We were just trying to get rid of the snake that fell out of the tree."

"A snake!" exclaimed Granddaddy. "Well why didn't you wake me up so I could have killed the snake?" he asked. "Don't you know that snake could have bit one of y'all?"

"Well, Jr. was the one that poured gas on it," said one of the boys.

"What gas?" asked my grandfather as he turned to look at my brother. Jr. as usual was standing there with a sheepish grin on his face and armed with a quick answer.

"Ummm, I knew you were tired and trying to get some rest. Then I remembered what you said about snakes and gas so, I just took care of it."

I could see that my grandfather was really amused with my brother's mischievousness but, he knew not to encourage him in his behavior. With a forced sternness in his voice, Granddaddy said "Boy, you could have been bit by that snake."

"No chance of that," said my brother proudly. "I was too quick for him."

"I tell you what," said Granddaddy. "Go up there and sit on the porch and don't move until I tell you to".

"Yes sir," said my brother. With slumped shoulders and a sad countenance on his face, Jr. climbed the four steps and took a seat on the edge of the porch.

Putting a little bass in his voice, my grandfather said, "Now you sit there and think about what you did."

"Yes sir," said my brother.

As my grandfather turned his back and walked away,

I could see a smile break out over his face. You see my grandfather was really a big kid at heart and my brother's antics were something he would have done as a child. But, he also knew that he had to hold my brother accountable for his actions. He needed to teach him that there are consequences for one's actions whether they be good or bad. Eventually, Granddaddy allowed my brother to go back and play with the rest of the boys and naturally they all thought he was the coolest dude of the group.

As I stood under the old oak tree watching my grandfather and my brother, I realized that the life lesson of accountability was being taught by my grandfather to his grandson. My grandparents are no longer living but that grand old oak is still standing.

THE ROAD MACHINE MAN

It was a hot August day and Granddaddy Van and I were standing in the field looking at the cotton. "Well, Peta," he said, "We got ourselves a good stand of cotton this year. Just look how thick it is. I should make a pretty good penny this year and if I do, I'll be able to pay some bills and buy y'all young ones some new high top shoes."

"Ugh," I thought to myself, "I really hate those ugly brown shoes."

Granddaddy stood proudly looking at his cotton field while relishing the thought of being able to make a little extra money in the near future for his family but, all I could see was missing the first few weeks of school and long rows of hot, hard cotton picking. Although these were my true feelings, I would never openly express them because I loved and respected my grandfather and would never take that proud moment from him.

Suddenly, we heard a roaring and scraping sound come down the dusty dirt road. I looked at Granddaddy and said, "That sounds like the road machine man." No sooner had I gotten the words out of my mouth, the road machine man came driving up.

Shrouded in a cloud of dust and black smoke bellowing from the pipe of his machine, the man jumped down and said "Howdy Van".

"Howdy to you, thank you," replied my grandfather.

Pulling a blue bandana handkerchief from the back pocket of his dingy blue overalls, the man wiped sweat from his forehead and said "It sure is hot today".

"It sure is," replied my grandfather.

"What you doing today?" the man asked my grandfather. "Well," replied Granddaddy, "me and my granddaughter were just out walking the fence line and checking on the fields. I was just telling her that I have a good stand of cotton this year."

Putting his hand over the top of his eyes as he scanned the fields, the man turned to my grandfather and said, "You sure have a nice place. Tell me, how many cows, mules and acres of land do you have here?"

Proudly looking at the man Granddaddy replied, "I have 15 cows, two mules and 80 acres of land."

Upon hearing this information, the man turned to Granddaddy and said, "Van, I been watching you over the years and you're a real good hard working feller. Tell you what I'm going to do for you. I'm going to make you a good deal on this here property. I'll give you ten thousand dollars for your house, land, cows and mules and I'll even allow you to live here until you die."

Tilting his head to the side with a quizzical look on his face, Granddaddy looked at the man and asked, "Do I look like a fool to you? I already own the land free and clear and besides I've been made to pay for it ten times over. Do you really think I'm gonna let you have my house and land and then you let me live in something I already own? A poor Negro just can't have nothing! Think you can offer me a few dollars and I will just jump at it. Tell you what," said my grandfather; "I think it's time for you to leave."

Thinking he had done my grandfather a big favor, the road machine man scratched his head and said "I don't know why you're so upset. I offered you a good deal."

"A good deal!" exclaimed my grandfather while waiving his hands in disgust. "What kind of deal is that? You gonna let me live in what I already own."

Realizing he had offended my grandfather, the man turned and hurriedly climbed back upon his machine. After carefully perching himself upon his seat, the man turned the engine of his contraption on, looked at my grandfather and said "You just can't help some folks." To show his contempt for my grandfather's rejection of his offer, the road machine man left without scraping our road.

"Well sir"! Exclaimed my grandfather. "How in the world did he think making an offer like that is helping me?" Shaking his head in disbelief, Granddaddy turned to me and said, "Peta, remember what I'm going to tell you this day. Some people in this world will tell you that you are nothing and that you shouldn't have certain things because you are Black, but I'm telling you that nobody is any better than you. Everybody is made out the same thing and that thing is spit and clay. Listen to me child and remember what I tell you. Granddaddy's not going to be with you always. But, promise me that when I'm gone you won't ever sell this land. I worked hard for this so my children and grandchildren could have their own and never be under the foot of any man again. Even if you leave home and go to the city, always pay the taxes and keep the land in the family, because you never know when you or your children may want to come back home. Always have your own so you don't have to beg nobody for a place to call home."

"Yes sir," I replied.

I was so proud of how my grandfather stood his ground but, at the same time I was afraid. This was during the turbulent Civil Rights Era and I thought, "That man is going to tell the Sheriff and then a lynch mob will come and kill my grandfather."

After teaching me this life lesson, Granddaddy looked down at me, held my hand, and said, "Let's go to the house." As we walked through the field to go home, I thought to myself, Granddaddy is my hero. Although he was a small man and short in stature, today he looked 10 feet tall because he stood up for his rights.

I remembered what my grandfather told me and kept my promise of keeping the land in the family. What he said those many years ago has come to pass because; several of his children and grandchildren have relocated to our homeland.

HOG KILLING TIME

October days had come, and the leaves had started to turn beautiful colors of red, orange, yellow, gold and brown. Looking up at the trees, I thought to myself, fall is such a beautiful time of the year. It's as if GOD took a paint brush and created a masterpiece with the leaves. "Peta," yelled Granddaddy Van, "stop day dreaming and get to picking up these sweet potatoes."

There was a chill in the air which made Granddaddy Van pull his flannel shirt close as he looked at me and said, "Come the first cold day, it will be hog killing time." Hog killing was an all day affair that usually took place in Granddaddy Israel's yard. This was the time when everyone in the community came together to perform the task of processing the butchered hogs. Not even the children were excluded from working on this day.

Earlier in the year, both of my grandfathers had chosen several hogs to be fattened up for the killing. There was a purifying procedure that took place before the hogs were killed. First, a pen was built and then a wooden floor was placed in the pen for the hogs to walk on. Only corn and a type of grass called puss were fed to the hogs. It was my job to make sure the hogs were fed and given water every evening. I can still hear Granddaddy Van saying, "Peta, you and Hub go pull some puss grass and feed them hogs". Ervin, affectionately called "Hub" by Granddaddy, would always stomp off and mumble that he was sick of pulling grass.

To keep him from getting in trouble, I would grab Earvin by the arm and say "Let's hurry so we can play before it gets dark." As the spring and summer passed, the hogs got fatter.

Finally one cold Saturday morning in November, Granddaddy came to our bed room and said, "Get up sleepy heads, it's hog killing time!" While we were trying to get our eyes opened, Mama Dora was busy making a fire in the stove so she could cook breakfast. We knew it would be a while before breakfast was ready so we decided to lay in bed a little longer. Sharon "aka" Shell stomped her foot on the floor. By doing this, she thought this would fool Granddaddy and make him think we were up. Now, Granddaddy being wise, was not fooled by Shell's ploy. He simply came to the door and said "If I have to call y'all again, I'm going to skin your hides.' Well that did it. We knew by the tone of his voice that he meant business this time. We all jumped up and started to get dressed.

Roy, better known as "Pee Wee," said, "Hog killing time is just too much work. Why do we have to do this anyway?"

"So we can have meat, silly," said Shell.

"Well," said Pee Wee, "it's still too much work. We have to go get wood to make a fire around the black pot, then we have to go back and forth to the spring to tote water to put in the pot, then after the hogs have been killed and butchered we have to help clean the chitterlings."

"Yuck!" said Shell, "You can keep them old stinking chitterlings."

"Yeah," I replied, "it's enough meat on the hog without having to keep the guts, feet, ears, snout, tail and the head. My goodness a poor hog don't stand a chance around here."

Suddenly, we heard Mama Dora say "Y'all chullens better come on and eat."

"Yes ma'am," we replied.

Breakfast at our grandparent's house usually consisted of a piece of fried dry salted pork, biscuits and rice with butter or fried pork fat poured over it. Sometimes it was just a bowl or cup of buttermilk and corn bread. Today it was the rice dish because it was going to be a long hard cold day. Man! Did that fried pork smell good. But to tell the truth, anything my grandmamma cooked was good to me.

"Hurry up and eat chullens, the day is half gone and besides, Van is waiting on us," said Mama Dora.

"Half gone," I thought while looking at the clock on the mantle-piece. "It's just 6:00 o'clock in the morning." Let me tell you, I may have thought this but I dared not say it out loud because back then that would have been considered as being sassy or talking back and children did not talk back to their elders.

Granddaddy Van, Granddaddy Israel and other men of the community had begun the hog killing process. They dug a hole in the ground, placed a large drum in it and then filled it with water. A fire was built around the drum in order to bring the water to a boil. While the water was getting hot, a familiar scene was taking place. My father had gone to the crib to get the maul so he could hit the hog(s) in the head.

"Bay," (my father's nick name), yelled Granddaddy Israel, "jump over in that hog pen and knock that big black sow out first."

"Yes sir," said my father. What a sight. As soon as Daddy jumped in the pen, the hog started running around in a circle while he ran behind her all the while swinging that maul.

Bam! Down fell Daddy in the mud. Immediately another man jumped in and continued the chase.

"Catch her! Catch her!" screamed all the children as they jumped up and down. Finally two of the men caught the hog and held her down while Daddy hit her in the head knocking it unconscious.

"Oh my goodness!" I cried. I felt so sorry for the poor thing.

"Go in the house if you can't stand it. Peta," said Granddaddy, "because, this is what we have to do if we want to have meat on the table. So just go in the house until I call you." With a hung down head and tears running down my cheeks, I went inside to wait for Granddaddy Van's call.

"Cry, cry, cry, you're always crying about something," I thought to myself. "You just can't stand anything, just such a crybaby." Answering myself, I said, "Well I can't help it if I have a soft heart. There should be a better way to kill the poor thing anyway."

While sitting there chastising myself, I heard my mother's kind and understanding voice saying, "Gwen stop crying and get back out there, This is just a part of life that must take place on the farm. We do what we have to do to make a living in this world and if you're ever going to make it, you have to grow a thicker skin."

"But it just doesn't seem fair to have to die like that," I said.

"Maybe not," she said, "but, life isn't always fair. We just have to work with the hand that is dealt us." Wiping my face, I got up and followed my mother outside.

As I walked around the corner of the house I saw the

men lift the hog and place it inside the barrel of hot water. The hot water would soften the hairs on the hog making it easier to scrape them off. Well wouldn't you know it, just as soon as that hog hit the hot water he became conscious and jumped out of the barrel.

"Run! Run!" I thought to myself. "Run for your life."

"Catch him! Catch him!" the grown-ups were yelling. "We can't let that meat get away."

What a frenzy, the hog was running for dear life, the men were running after the hog, the dogs were running after the men, the women were screaming and the children were laughing at the sight of it all. Eventually, the hog was caught and slaughtered and the hard work of preparing the meat took place. Everyone toiled and labored together in peace, love and harmony doing what was necessary to feed their families. When the work was finally finished, every household in the community was given a share of the meat. Absolutely no one was left out. While lying in bed exhausted from the day's work, I replayed the scene of my father falling while chasing the hog. I chuckled at the thought, silently whispered my prayers and fell asleep.

As I think about those days of old, I realize just how blessed I am to have been reared in a community where everyone supported and looked out for each other.

THE TOM CAT

It was a cold Sunday morning. Everyone was still in bed exhausted from the previous day of hard work during the hog killing. Suddenly there was a sound on the roof. It was an awful but familiar growling and scratching made by a stray tom cat that had come into our community. I don't know why, but for some reason, the cat had prowled around our house all summer. He would make frightening growling noises and scratch and claw on the doors. At night, the cat would climb on top of our house and try to come down the side of the chimney that led into our bedroom.

During the previous winter, the stove pipe of our wood burning heater had gotten too hot and the roof around the pipe had burned. This left a hole in the ceiling. For some reason unknown to us, the cat became obsessed with trying to enter our home through that hole. My mother had taken old quilts and rags and stuffed them in the hole in order to keep the cat out.

On one occasion, the cat had actually gotten half way into our room. That was a very scary night. My sister and I awoke to a growling noise. It was very dark and we couldn't see so we just started screaming "Daddy! Daddy!" My father and mother ran into our room and pulled the light string.

"What in the world is going on?" asked my mother.

"By the heater!, by the heater!," we screamed. "We heard growling by the heater". My father looked up and there was the cat. He had backed half way down the side of the chimney.

"What the world!!" exclaimed, my father. My mother grabbed the broom and started beating the cat. Back up through the roof he went. Daddy ran to get his gun but the cat had gotten away.

"Oh my goodness," said my mother. "You have got to get this roof fixed and you have got to do something about that cat".

"I know," said my father, nodding his head in agreement. At this point, my father had become very frustrated with having to run the cat away. So he said, "I am going to fix that cat once and for all."

Well, just like clockwork, the cat came back the next evening. We didn't have screen doors and my mother had left the kitchen door open to let smoke out of the house that came from the wood burning stove. Wouldn't you know it, that old cat climbed up the steps, ran through the open door and jumped on top of the deep freezer. Daddy had been waiting for him. He had put a boiler of water on the stove and let it come to a roaring boil and then he went and hid behind the kitchen door. As soon as the cat jumped on the deep freezer, my father hit him with a stick and the cat fell behind the freezer. My father, thinking he had knocked the cat out, reached behind the freezer to pull him out. What a mistake that was. That old cat latched onto my father's hand and boy oh boy what a fiasco. Daddy was running around yelling and screaming, "Get him off! Get him off!" And the cat was growling, scratching and clawing his hand and arm.

Daddy jumped out the back door and everybody in the house ran right out behind him yelling and screaming. My mother grabbed the pot of hot water and called to my father "Sling him off and I'll pour the water on him."

"That's what I'm trying to do," yelled my father. After

what seemed like hours of fighting with the cat, Daddy finally realized that he was still holding the stick, so he took it, hit the cat on the head and it immediately fell to the ground. As soon as he hit the ground, my mother was right there with the hot water and dashed it on the cat. What a sight, the cat jumped up and ran into the woods and my poor father's arm was bleeding and scratched to ribbons. My mother took my father by the hand, led him into the house, cleaned and then bandaged his wounds. After everything had settled down, my father rubbed his arm and said, "That was one tough cat but, we got the best of him. I don't think he'll come back around here anymore."

    Finally, the tom cat nightmare was over and for the first time in a long time, we all had a peaceful night's sleep. I've often wondered where the tom cat came from and why he targeted our house, but I'm happy to say that we never saw him again. I will forever remember by father gallantly defending his family from that mean old tom cat.

THE CHRISTMAS TREE HUNT

Thanksgiving was over, the last of the turkey and dressing had been eaten and the only thing left was a piece of jelly cake. Mom was busy cleaning up the kitchen when she turned and said, "Time to wash your feet and get ready for bed children, tomorrow you must start looking for a Christmas tree so, you better get a good night's sleep."

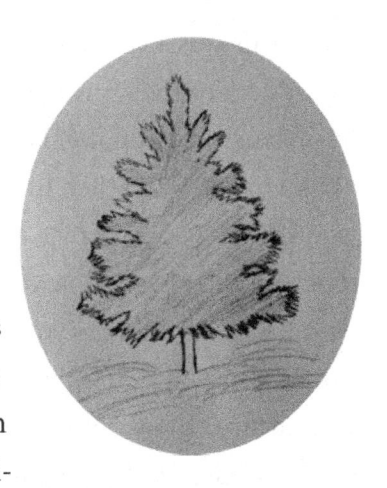

Christmas tree hunting was a big event for us. All of the children in the neighborhood would get together and search the woods, fields and pastures of the entire Moore Place Community. This event always took place on a Saturday. It was a joyous occasion. There was singing of Christmas Carols and sharing wishes of the toys we hoped to get from Santa Claus.

I was the first to wash my feet and put my night clothes on, then Shell, Jr. and finally Donnie got his turn. I was always first because I was the oldest and because, I didn't want to wash in water after other people. Shell and I shared a bed and Jr. and Donnie slept on a pleather (which is my definition for fake leather) sofa that converted into a bed. On really cold nights, all four of us slept in the same bed. Times were hard for us, but God always brought us through. After we were all dressed and ready for bed, we said our prayers and then Mom gave each of us a blanket. We took our blankets and then waited for my mother to turn the covers down on the bed. Our house was old and very cold. It had pine knot holes in the wall and a leaky tin roof. This was a very cold November Friday night so naturally, we all slept in the same bed. Our mother took extra measures to keep us warm on nights like this. She would give each one of us a blanket and then line us up in front of the potbellied wood burning heater that stood in the corner. One by one she took each blanket and held it to the heater until it was nice and warm. She would wrap you in it and then you would take a running start and jump in the bed with your blanket wrapped around you. To us this was fun but to my mother it was a necessary procedure in keeping us warm. As we ran to jump in the bed, the giggling was on. Mom covered us up, gave each one of us a good night kiss and then turned the lights out. As she was leaving the room, she turned and said "Mama loves you babies." These were always the last words she said to us every night before we went to sleep.

As soon as she left the room, we started whispering about what kind of tree we would find, the type of decorations we would make and what we hoped Santa would bring us this year. My mother heard us and said, "Stop that talking and go to sleep."

"Yes Ma'ammm!" we replied. All was quiet until Jr. let out a giggle and then we all started to giggle.

"Be quiet!" I said, "Mom is going to get us."

"Ok, ok," said Shell. All is quiet and then Shell giggled and then we all start giggling again.

By this time, Mom came to the door and said, "If I have to tell y'all one more time to be quiet, I'm going to spank all of you and you won't be going to look for a tree tomorrow." Well, that broke up the giggling because, we knew by the tone of her voice that she was serious this time.

Cock-a-doddle-do the rooster crows. "Wake up!" I yelled excitedly. "It's time to go tree hunting."

"Not yet," said my mother. "It's too early."

"Good grief", I thought! "Well let's just go back to sleep," said Shell. Mom made our standard breakfast which consisted of biscuits, buttered rice and dry salted meat.

After eating and cleaning up the kitchen, it was time to embark on our tree hunting journey. The hunt usually took place around noon. Eventually, all of the children gathered in our front yard and off we went to look for a tree. Up the road we went, laughing, talking, running and jumping. We went over the hills, down in the valleys, through pastures and into the woods looking for the right tree. What great fun we were having when out of nowhere some horses came running after us. At that point, it was every child for him or herself. Some climbed trees and some hid in bushes. I was lucky enough to find a tree with a low limb and up I climbed. My heart was beating so fast and I could hardly breathe.

"Is everyone safe?" one of my cousins shouted.

"Yes," we all answered. The horses stood under the trees for a while and then left. We waited for a few minutes to make sure they were gone before climbing down.

"Who's horses are those and where did they come from?" I asked.

"I don't know," said one of my cousins.

"Well I think they are gone," said my sister. So we all climbed down and as soon we hit the ground, the horses came charging after us again. Everyone started screaming and we ran as fast as we could to the wire fence that was enclosed around the woods. Most of the children climbed over the fence, but I hit the ground and rolled under it. Once safely on the other side, I looked back and said, "Whew! That was close."

Although the incident was scary, it did not stop us from finding our tree. We merrily continued on our quest and what do you know? I found the perfect tree in Uncle Jerry's pasture. Eventually, everyone found their tree, marked it for later when we would return to cut it down and then it was time to go home. We all got back on the main road and headed for home. What a story we had to tell our parents about our encounter with the wild and crazy horses when we got home. As I think back over the incident, I'm pretty sure the horses were not wild and really meant us no harm. But, when you are a child your imagination will make you believe things that are probably not true.

The Christmas holidays have become so commercialized until the true essence of the season, which is celebrating the birth of **JESUS**, has been lost. Store bought ornaments and artificial trees are the norm and real trees are rarely used. But I am so thankful for the beautiful memories of the Christmas traditions of my childhood.

SANTA CLAUS AND THE AIRPLANE

It was Christmas Eve and everybody was excited because this was the night that Santa would come. Ma-dear was busy in the kitchen cooking; Daddy was chopping fire wood for the night and Shell and I had the chore of bringing the wood into the house. "Daddy"! exclaimed Shell, "you need to hurry up and finish because we have to go to bed so Santa Claus can come."

"Don't worry about it," said Daddy. "We'll finish in time". Suddenly a rain drop fell.

"Is that rain?" asked Shell.

"Don't worry about it," said Daddy again. "Just do your work."

Slowly the rain increased and my poor sister became really alarmed. She began to cry and asked, "What will Santa do if it keeps raining? Surely he won't be able to see how to fly his sleigh with reindeers in the rain."

"Remember Rudolph's red nose?" I said. "He'll be able to see."

"But what about the open sleigh?" she asked. "Won't he get wet? Won't the toys get wet?"

Seeing that my sister was really upset, my mother said, "Don't worry, if it starts to rain really hard then Santa will come in an airplane." Mom's explanation seemed to calm her down and she resumed her chore of taking wood into the house.

As luck would have it, an airplane flying really low, came across the house as we were picking up our last stack of wood in the yard. "Ahhhhhh!!!" screamed Shell as she threw down her armful of wood and ran into my mother's arms. "Santa is here and we haven't said our prayers and gone to bed yet. Now we won't get any toys and Santa is going to spit snuff in our eyes," she said.

"That's not true," I said. "And anyway why would he spit snuff in your eyes?"

"Because," said Shell, "I'm not asleep. That's why."

"For goodness sake," I said, "Santa can see that we are working, so he'll just go to the other children's houses and then come back to us when we go to sleep."

"That's right", said my mother. "Now stop crying and finish your work."

Finally our chores were done. We then took our shoe boxes, wrote our names on them and carefully placed them under the Christmas tree. We didn't have stockings to hang by the fireplace so we used shoe boxes. And, if we didn't get new shoes that year, we would take a brown paper bag, roll the top down about three times and use that as our stocking. Personally, I liked the shoe box better because it was bigger and there was room for more stuff. "Now," said my mother, "take your baths and put on your night clothes so you can get into bed." "Yes ma'am," we both said.

Shell turned to me and said, "Oh, I wonder what will we get for Christmas this year?"

"I don't know," I said , "but, I sure hope we both get our own doll. Last year we had to share a doll."

"I hope so too," said my sister.

"Have you girls finished dressing for bed?" asked my mother.

"Yes ma'am," we both said.

"Well, say your prayers and then bring me your blankets."

"Yes ma'am!!" we said, as we giggled and pushed each other. While we were dressing, my mother had turned down the covers on our old wrought iron bed. It was really cold that Christmas Eve. As a matter of fact, it had actually started sleeting outside.

"Girls! you don't have all night," said my mother. "You had better get in here and go to bed so Santa can come and bring your toys."

"Here we come," I said.

We both grabbed our blankets and ran to my mother. She took Shell's blanket, held it to the old pot bellied heater to warm it and then wrapped it around her. Then, it was my turn.

"Now hurry to bed before your blankets get cold," said my mother. We both took a running start and jumped into bed. My mother tucked us in, gave us both a kiss and whispered, "Mama loves you babies."

"We love you too," we both replied. My mother pulled the light string that hung from the exposed light socket hanging from the ceiling.

All was quiet and dark when suddenly another airplane could be heard in the distance. My sister went into full panic mode. She jumped out of the bed and started screaming, "Here comes Santa and we're not sleep."

At this point my father came in our bedroom to reassure her that everything was ok and that it was not Santa's airplane. My sister calmed down and we eventually fell asleep.

Finally it was Christmas morning and our wish came

true. We both got our very own plastic doll with hair that we could comb. This was truly special because the doll we got the prior year had plastic hair and to make matters worse, we had to share it. Also in our box were two apples, two oranges, some raisins on the vine, three Brazil nuts, three walnuts and some hard candy. We ate the contents very slowly because Christmas was the only time of year that we received store bought fruits and nuts so we had to make it last. What a wonderful day it was. To my sister and I, it was the best Christmas ever.

    As I look back over the years and recall that very special Christmas of long ago, I can still see the joy on my parents face as they watched their two little girls playing with their dolls by the Christmas tree. And, to this very day, whenever it rains on Christmas Eve, I still remember Santa Claus and his airplane.

THE WALKING ENCYCLOPEDIA

My baby brother Donnie, whose proper name is Israel Donnell Moore, III, has always been a very intellectual child. As a toddler, he never really played very much. My older brother along with other kids in the neighborhood was always asking him to come outside. Sometimes he would take them up on their request but, if engrossed in his favorite pastime of reading, the reply would be, "Nah maybe another time." To be honest, he was the only child I knew that spent his leisure time looking in encyclopedias, magazines and news papers. Because of his intense interest in the encyclopedia, it actually inspired the rest of us to start reading the thing. There were many a rainy days when we couldn't go outside that we spent playing name the state flower, bird and capitol of each state from the encyclopedia. For each correct answer, you earned a point and lost a point for an incorrect answer. The person with the most points at the end of the game was the winner.

Although Donnie was an voracious reader, listening to the radio and watching the Romper Room, Captain Kangaroo and commercials on the television were his true passion. I can still see him quietly sitting in front of that old black and white RCA Victor television in our humble little home. We didn't know just how much he was learning from watching television until one summer when my uncle and aunt from Las Vegas came for a visit. It was my aunt that noticed him reading the items on the shelves while she and my mother were in the grocery store. Because he was only four years old at the time, she thought surely this child can't be reading. Determined to find out if he truly was, she began to point to different products on the shelf and ask what is this? To her surprise, he answered correctly every time.

Shaking her head in total disbelief, my aunt exclaimed, "What in the world is this Leola got on her hand?" "Here," she said, lifting Donnie out of the grocery cart and handing him to my mother, "Take him away from me. I've never known a baby that could read at this age."

"Whatever are you talking about?" asked my mother. "This child can't read."

"Oh yes he can," said my aunt. 'Just watch this". Pointing to a box of washing powder sitting on the shelf, she asked "What is the name on this box Darnell?"

Taking a few minutes to examine the product, my brother calmly said, "That's Cheer."

With an astounded look on her face, my mother asked "What the world? How long have you been reading and who taught you?"

Because he was a child, Donnie did not understand why his ability to read was such a big deal. He just looked at Mom with a quizzical look on his face, shrugged his shoulders and answered, "From the TV."

"Well, I declare," replied my mother;" I sure didn't know you could read."

"Told you so," said my aunt. "That boy's going far in this world."

From that moment of discovery all the way to this present day, my brother is constantly reading and discovering new things. He became a collector of Archie Comic Books, Match Box cars and a dedicated listener of every PBS and World News station there is. Whenever you visit him, there is always some kind of short wave radio playing. There is absolutely no subject you mention that he can't tell you something about it. If he can't give you an answer at that moment, he'll say give me a minute and I'll get back with you. Be assured, he will get an answer for you. Because he is so knowledgeable about every social issue, he is often referred to by family and friends as the walking encyclopedia. The common theme among everyone that knows him is, if you have a question about anything just ask Donnie.

    My brother shared his love of the encyclopedia with my daughter by giving her a complete set of World Book Encyclopedias for her twelfth birthday. Also, his sons have inherited his love of collecting Match Box Cars.

GHOST IN THE CLOAK ROOM

It was a cold January day and we had spent the night with Mama Dora and Granddaddy Van. As we were walking to Bethel Hill School, the ground that we walked on crunched under our feet. The frost was as white as snow and ice cycles spewed up out of the ground. The water puddles on the side of the dirt road were frozen solid. Clarence, Charlie, Earvin and I were laughing and talking when suddenly we decided to take a running start and skate on the frozen puddles. Bam!!! Down I fell and bumped the back of my head. Everyone thought that was funny except me because the fall really gave me a headache. Earvin helped me up and we walked on to school. When we got there, our teacher Ms. Clay had made a fire in the pot-bellied heater. We all raced to it to get warm. One of the older children had gone to the coal pile and bought coal in and started the fire for Ms. Clay.

It was so cold that day until we had to place our chairs in a circle around that old heater in order to keep warm. There was a stage in the class room and in order to get to the blackboard, you had to walk across the stage. It was actually too cold to go to the blackboard so we just sat around the heater and read books. The first graders were reading "Spot". All day long it was run Spot run, see Spot run. "Boy oh boy," I thought to myself, "Spot should really get tired of running." The 2nd and 3rd graders were reading Jack and Janet and I don't know what the older kids were reading. There was a second room with an old piano in it.

While sitting there quietly reading our books, the piano started playing. We were afraid because one of the older boys said that a ghost was playing the piano. Ms. Clay threw up her hands in exasperation and said, "There is no such thing as ghosts and besides, it's probably just a mouse running across the keys."

Then, we heard the sound of footsteps walking in the cloak room. Well don't you know the screaming was on.

"Be quiet children," said Ms. Clay. "It's probably just the wind blowing the shutters and making them bang against the window." In order to calm us down, Ms. Clay told us to get back in our seats and then she went in the room to investigate.

As soon as Ms. Clay stepped out of the classroom, Charlie jumped out of his seat, placed his hands on his cheeks and said, "What if she doesn't come back? What will happen to us? The ghost will probably get all of us!"

"Shut up Charlie! And be quiet," I said. "You're always starting something.'"

"Ha, ha, ha, ha," laughed Charlie while pointing his finger at me. "You're scared, you're scared, ha, ha, ha, Gwen is scared."

"I am not!" I shot back at him. "I just want you to shut up."

Finally Ms. Clay came back into the classroom and said "See, I told you there was nothing to be afraid of. It was just the wind blowing the shutters in the cloak room like I told you. Now get back to reading."

Charlie leaned over and whispered, "Hey Gwen, I still think it was a ghost because she didn't say what made the piano play."

"Twelve o'clock, lunch time," said Ms. Clay.

My cousin Sand leaned over and asked, "Gwen, what did you bring today?"

"Oh just some peanuts and a sugar and butter biscuit," I said. My brown paper bag had grease spots on it where the butter had melted and stained it.

Earvin sighed and said, "I get tired of sugar and butter biscuits. Why can't we have something else sometimes?"

I looked at him and said, "Well at least we have something to eat. Some children don't have anything."

Earvin shrugged his shoulders and said, "I guess you're right."

Ms. Clay had placed and old coffee can with some water in it and two eggs on top of the pot-bellied heater. Two boiled eggs was what she had for lunch. Although Ms. Clay was a teacher, she was poor just like the rest of us. Teachers were not paid very much in those days. I loved Ms. Clay; she was a very caring and jolly teacher that loved the students as if they were her own children. At recess or lunch-time, she would play softball with the children but, not today because it was much too cold to play outside.

"Well children," said Miss Clay "since we can't go outside today, I guess I will tell you all a story."

"How about The Three Little Pigs?" said one of the first graders.

"Three pigs," said Charlie. "That's for babies. Let's have a ghost story."

"Shut up Charlie!" I said, "you just never quit."

"Ha, ha, ha, still scared are we?" asked Charlie, while

pointing his finger at me again.

"No I am not, but you are scaring the little kids," I said.

"Okay children that's enough," said Miss Clay. "I tell you what; since you all can't decide, just lay your heads on your desk and take a nap."

"Happy now Mr. big mouth?" asked one of the kids.

"Oh shut up," snapped Charlie, "I was just playing."

All was quiet when suddenly we hear a noise in the cloakroom room again, bam! bam! bam!. Everybody jumped up screaming and ran straight to Miss Clay. Even Charlie is shaken this time. Startled and half asleep herself, Miss Clay jumps out of her chair and yells, "What is the matter with you children?"

"The ghost is back! The ghost is back!" everyone yelled. "We heard it knocking in the cloak room."

"What are you talking about?" said Miss Clay. "I told you there is no such thing as ghosts. Now go back to your seats."

"Please Miss Clay," asked one of the small children while crying, "can't we just go home? I'm really scared."

"Oh goodness we might as well," she said. "Besides it's too cold in here anyway."

"Thank goodness!" I thought to myself, "I just want to go home."

"Listen children," said Miss. Clay, "put your books away, straighten your chairs up and let's line up and go to the cloak room to get our coats". Everyone lined up and Miss Clay took the lead, As she opened the door of our classroom, the cloak room door was standing wide open. Paper was scattered everywhere and all of our coats were on the floor. Everyone gasped and one of the children asked what happened.

"I don't know," said Miss Clay, "but I'm sure it was just the wind, now pick up your coats and put them on. Girls, tie your heads up, boys, put your hats on and hurry home out of this cold."

"Yes ma'am!," we said and quietly did as we were told.

"Now don't tarry and tell your parents I let you out early because of the cold weather."

"Yes ma'am!" we all replied.

As I was walking down the path that led from the school, I looked back. Miss Clay was standing in the door with a look on her face that I had never seen before. She too was clearly shaken. We never knew what really happen at school that day. Perhaps a mouse did run across the keys of the piano and maybe the wind did ramshackle the cloak room and blow our coats on the floor. But, maybe it really was a ghost in the cloak room that day. I guess we'll never really know.

Bethel Hill School is no longer there, but it is listed on the USGS National Mapping Information as historical. Whenever I visit the location where it stood, the memory of my sweet teacher and our encounter with the cloakroom ghost still brings a smile to my face.

OLD COON UP THE TREE

Granddaddy Van was a very avid and legendary coon hunter. To put it mildly, he was the best there was in Sumter County. He was so respected for his hunting skills until all of the older White men in our county would bring their sons to be trained by him. And, naturally all of the young men in our neighborhood at some point in their lives went on a hunting adventure with my grandfather. He was also very well versed in the ways of coons and their behavior. He would often talk to us about how a coon would stay up in a tree for hours feeding on wild grapes, persimmons and acorns. He had four coon hounds that according to him were the best dogs in the world. There was a Blue Tick Hound name Hitler, a Walker Hound name Spot and two Black and Tan Hounds named Lig and Old Dan. They were the best he said, because any one of his dogs could catch wind of a coon laying up in a tree without ever smelling a track on the ground. "As a matter of fact," he said, "they were so smart until they had sense enough to bark repeatedly on a cold track but, would stop barking when the track got hot and just sneak up on that old coon and tree him every time."

Granddaddy and his dogs were so in sync with each other until he could tell what they were tracking by the sound of their bark. He said if old Lig was tracking cold and then hot and running back and forth up the river bank then he was surley on the trail of a mink. And if old Spot was tracking and started running around in circles near thick weeds then he was trailing a rabbit. Granddaddy said coons were smart and very hard to fool down out of a tree. He said an old seasoned one would sit with his face turned up at the moon and no matter how much you shined the light on him or how loud the dogs barked and ran around the tree, he was not coming down. But, that was not the case in this following hunting escapade that occurred when Granddaddy took my brother Walter, Jr. hunting.

It was a cold fall night and we were all sitting around the fireplace eating roasted sweet potatoes that Mama Dora had just raked from the ashes. While brushing ash from the potato in his hand, Granddaddy informed Mama Dora that he was going to take my brother Jr. coon hunting with him.

"Grandson," he said to my brother, "you worked hard helping Granddaddy work on the fence line today so I'm going to take you hunting tonight. We gonna catch us a big old coon for your grandmother to cook for us tomorrow. I can see him now just laid up there all roasted with sweet potatoes round him."

"Yes sir!!' my brother said with his usual sheepish grin on his face.

"Van," said Mama Dora, "it's mighty cold to be taking that child out there to go hunting."

"Awh Dora he'll be alright," said Granddaddy. "This will just make a man out of him. Go in there boy and get ready," said Granddaddy. "We going to get us a coon tonight."

"Yes sir," replied my brother, as he ran into the back bedroom to get dressed.

"You better bundle up real good," said my grandmother, "and be sure to put on your long hammers."

"I will," said my brother.

"Van," said Mama Dora, "you better take care of that boy and don't let him get hurt."

Granddaddy just looked at Mama, made a grunting noise and said, "Come on boy, get your gun and let's go."

What a grand and proud figure my brother cut when he stepped out of the back room. He had his hunting lantern strapped around his head, his hunting boots on and his gun slung across his shoulder. In that moment, I realized that my little brother was growing up. My siblings were like my children to me and I was every bit as worried for his safety as my grandmother was. It was dusk dark when Jr. and my grandfather stepped down off the porch. As I followed them outside, I asked my brother if he was scared. "Naw," said my brother, "I'm with Granddaddy." In our eyes, Granddaddy was invincible and as long as we were with him, we felt that nothing could hurt us.

"Van, you take care of that boy," said my grandmother.

"Stop worrying Dora," he said. "I know what I'm doing."

Granddaddy went around to the back of the house and unchained his coon dogs, Old Dan and Spot. "Let's go get us a coon boys", he said to his dogs. As if they understood what he was saying, the dogs started barking and jumping on Granddaddy's leg. Off they went down the road, Granddaddy, my brother and the two dogs. The lanterns on Granddaddy and Jr.'s heads made them look like aliens.

I thought to myself, "If I was a coon and saw that coming towards me, I wouldn't come down out the tree either." I stood on the porch and watched my brother and grandfather until they were out of sight.

"Come on in the house child," said my grandmother to me. "Don't worry they'll be back directly."

As I turned to go into the house, a blast of cold air brushed over me which made me scamper really fast back inside. I walked over to the fireplace, stretched my hands forward to warm myself and whispered a prayer for my beloved grandfather and brother's safety.

This is what happened according to my brother: Granddaddy and Jr. waded through the remaining corn stalks that were still standing in the field and across the road onto the other side of our property. The dogs started barking and on and on they went until they came upon a big persimmon tree that stood right in the middle of an old abandoned grave yard. Around and around the tree the dogs ran. Then, they started barking and jumping upon the side of the tree just scratching like they were trying to climb it.

"Shine the light up in the tree boy," said my grandfather. "We got us one now." Jr. did as he was told and shined the light in the tree. According to him when he shinned the light all he saw was something with a big wide back like a man. He said when the light struck the back of the supposed coon, it slowly turned it's head around and what he saw up in that tree was definitely not a coon. What he saw in the tree had big round red eyes that just glared down at him. Then, what ever it was jumped down on the ground with a loud thud and the dogs went silent.

My brother said when he turned to run towards my grandfather his feet would not move. The only thing that snapped him out of his trance was the dog that ran between his legs and knocked him down.

"Granddaddy! Granddaddy!" yelled my brother, "It ain't no coon. I don't know what it is, but believe me it sure ain't no coon."

My brother said Granddaddy let out a yell and said, "Run boy, run, get up and run."

Finally my brother was able to get up. My grandfather started running, my brother started running and the dogs just ran off and left them. My brother said Granddaddy was running so fast until all he could say was, "Wait Granddaddy, wait."

He said Granddaddy looked back over his shoulder and said, "You better keep up boy." In desperation, my brother said he reached out and grabbed Granddaddy's coat tail. He said they were running so fast he could hardly breath and the only thing he could hear was Granddaddy saying, "Turn my coat loose boy and run."

Down through the grave yard and out through the woods they ran. The dogs were no where in sight. Finally after what seemed like an eternity, they made it back to the road and were able to stop running. Clutching his chest while gasping for air, my brother turned to Granddaddy and asked, "What in the world was that? And, what happened to the dogs? They just ran of and left us."

"I don't know," replied Granddaddy, "but whatever you do don't tell Dora cause, I will never hear the end of it."

"I won't tell it," said my brother. After composing themselves, Jr. and Granddaddy started walking back home. Every so often they would look back to make sure they were not being followed by that grand old coon that did come down out of the tree.

My brother kept his word and never told my grandmother about the incident. But, he did share his hunting secret with me. Whenever we have a family gathering, he always tell the story about the coon that came down out of the tree.

A CRY FOR HELP

Life was sometimes hard for my family. Money was scarce and often time there was not enough to pay all the bills. In the early years of my parents marriage, my father was the main bread winner and my mother was a stay at home mom. This was back in the early fifties and the only work available to Black women in rural Alabama where we lived was housekeeping for a well-to-do White family or working in the fields picking cotton. There was only one car in our family which my father used to go to work. Therefore working outside of the home for my mother was not an option. My father worked at the local lumber mill in the town of Bellamy, Alabama. The work was hard and the pay was small. The lumber mill where my father worked had a commissary in which the employees could set up a charge account to purchase food, clothing and other items against their salaries. Sometimes on pay day, my father's checks would be so small until it seemed as if he was working for free.

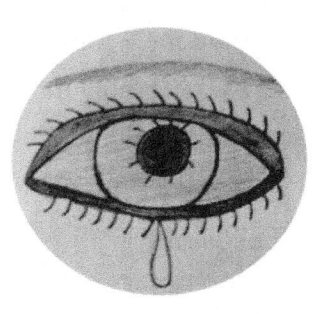

I remember on one occasion, my father came home one Friday evening and gave my mother five ($5.00) dollars and told her to take it and buy groceries and bring him the change. She asked him why so little money and he replied "Because, I bought groceries over the past weeks and they told me it took all my pay except $5.00."

My mother sighed and said "Surely that little food you bought home last week could not have cost enough to take most of your check."

My father hung his head in dismay and said "That's what

they told me." Although my father felt this was not accurate, there was nothing he could do about it because questioning his employer could possibly have cost him his job.

Over the next few years my mother obtained her G.E.D. and finally got a job at the local hospital as a cook. The pay was minimum wage but it was better than not being employed. Both my parents were now working but they were still struggling. At night when my mother thought everyone was asleep, I would often hear her praying and crying out to the Lord for help. I could hear her saying, "Lord if you don't help me I don't know what we are going to do. My children need shoes and clothes, the light bill is due, the insurance is due and I only have a few dollars to work with. Lord have mercy on us".

Hearing my mother cry at night would make my sister and me sad and we would cry for her. Sometimes we would cry ourselves to sleep. My mother never knew that we would hear her crying for help at night. At one point during my childhood, things got so bad until my mother wrote a letter to our State Senator asking for help. My father had fallen ill from a stroke and things really got bad for us. Because I was the oldest child, my mother would talk to me about our financial situation. She said I have done all that I can possibly do and now I have decided to write to our Senator for help. So on November 20, 1974, my mother wrote the following letter:

Dear Senator:

I am Mrs. Leola S. Moore, the wife of Mr. Walter E. Moore, the mother of 4 children. I am writing this letter in the regards of my family. My husband has been ill since November 28, 1973. Up until this present time he has been totally disabled to work, he was a employee at the local Lumber Mill for over 20 years

and since he been sick he has not been able to draw any kind of unemployment or workman compensation, nor disability or Social Security. I have filed 3 times and each time he was denied. The Dr's say he has Hypertensive crisis; cardiovascular disease. I have taken him to 3 hospitals and each Dr. came up with the same diagnosis, yet I have not been able to receive any help for him. I work at a hospital making $1.90 per hour and 80 hours every two weeks my net pay is $285.58 per month plus I get a A.D.C. check for four children at $112 per month a total of $397.58 coming into the house a month. I am sending a list of some of the bills I have to facing each month. A lot of bills my husband owed before he got sick, the people are beginning to try to hold me responsible for paying them. They are threatening my job by calling me at work or writing my administrator asking him about my paying the bill, but I am just not able. Also, the Internal Revenue has wrote me a letter saying if I didn't pay the whole amount of income tax we owe back at once, they will serve a levy on my employer, bank account, receivables, commissions, property or any other belongings of mine will be seized. When I pay a little on all these bill, we don't have food to eat. Right now my children need shoes to wear to school. So please if there is any way you can, help me please.
Thank you.
THE FOLLOWING IS A LIST OF MY MONTHLY HOUSE HOLD BILLS

Car Note..$100.00
Balance of my husband's Dr. Bill..................... $199.07
House Note... $ 65.00
United Insurance.. $ 9.12
Sears/Roebuck..$ 15.00

Fairfax Loan Co........................ ....$ 31.00
Light Bill... $ 17.88 more/ less
Car Insurance.. $ 28.00
Telephone Bill.. $ 14.62
Western Auto............... .... $ 27.00
Mortgage Insurance...................................... $ 15.61
Spiegel... $ 10.00
TOTAL BILLS................. .... $532.30
This does not include gas for car to go to work, butane gas for house, general household supplies nor food.

Very Truly Yours,
Mrs. Walter Moore.

    My mother did not have access to a copier so she wrote a duplicate of her original letter. She mailed one copy and kept the other copy in her files. I still have her hand written copy of the above letter.

TEAM WORK

It had been well over a year since my mother wrote her letter to our State Senator, but yet no reply. I would watch her as she faithfully checked the mail box each and every day. Finally realizing that her desprate plea had not been heard, Mom stopped going to the mailbox. Having been the main bread winner for our family for so many years, my father was becoming very anxious about our financial situation. He held his head in his hands and asked "Leola, what are we going to do?"

Seeing the desperation in his eyes and the despair in his voice, my mother reassured him that everything would be alright. She took his hand and calmly told him, "Don't worry Bay, we'll get by with the help of the Lord."

Regardless of our situation, my mother never lost her faith. Late that night after everyone had gone to bed, I heard my mother get up and quietly go to the bathroom. She was careful not to wake my father because she did not want him to get upset. I could hear her praying and asking GOD to please give her the strength to take care of her family. After several minutes of praying, she came to me and my sister's bedroom, rubbed and kissed each of our foreheads and said, "Lord please take care of my children." I wanted to reach out and hug my mother and tell her I loved her but, because I was supposed to be asleep, I could not do so. After leaving our room, she entered the boy's room and repeated the same routine with them and then quietly climbed back into her bed. My heart broke for my mother and the only thing I knew to do was pray that GOD would help her.

Several days later while sitting around the dinner table, Mom had a serious talk with us about our situation. She said, "I don't make very much money working as a cook at the hospital and due to your father having a stroke, he is no longer able to work. Therefore, things are pretty tight right now but, we can make it through this storm if we work together as a team." My mother instructed us to all hold hands as she prayed for her family. Upon completion of her prayer she said "Now, I want you all to always remember when you leave this house, hold your heads up high and keep a smile on your face. We may have to eat buttermilk and corn bread for a while but if it comes to that then so be it. And, if we have to cry all night, then we'll cry but when morning comes, we will thank GOD for another day, wash our faces, put on a smile and face our trials with a new determination. But," she said, "I want you all to know that this too shall pass and we will survive. Remember children, the race is not given to the swift nor the strong, but to the one that endureth to the end. Now," she said again, "in order for us to survive, "Gwen you and Shell are going to have to get a job."

"Yes ma'am!" we readily replied. "But where?" we asked?

" I don't know yet but the LORD will send something our way," she said.

I was 19 years old at the time and my sister was 16. Not wanting to be over looked, my brothers Jr. who was 13 and Donnie who was 12 asked, "What about us? We want to help too".

Not wanting to crush their spirits, my mother said "I know you want to help but you are both too young to get a public job. But, you can still help by doing chores around the house like washing the dishes, folding clothes and sweeping the floor."

"What!" exclaimed my brother Jr. with a frown on his face. "That's girls work. Boys don't do that kind of stuff."

"Hey son,," stated my father, "don't talk back to your mother. If she say wash dishes then that's what you'll do."

" Yes sir," replied my brother.

Although Jr. did not say anything else, I knew that wasn't the end of the story for him. There was no way he was going to settle for washing dishes and sweeping floors while his sisters did public work. After my father left the room, Jr. approached our mother and asked if she would talk to her supervisor about him doing yard work around her house. "Alright son" she replied, "I will." The next day, my mother came home with news that not only had her supervisor agreed to hire Jr. to do yard work, she also recommended my sister as a weekend house keeper and baby sitter for one of her friends. I had also secured a job as a waitress at the local restaurant. Trying to maintain our school work, chores and a job was very difficult but, we did what we had to do. Upon receipt of our first check, we were all smiles because we were able to contribute to the support of our family. My mother was right, by working together as a team, we were able to survive and boy oh boy what an awesome team we were.

As the years passed, Donnie became of age and landed a job at the local grocery store. Jr. secured a second job working for the local nursery on weekends, I gained work study at the University between classes in addition to my waitress job and Shell continued her house keeping and baby sitting job. Regardless of how difficult times were for us, my mother always insisted that we keep a portion of our earnings. She would give each one of us a hug and say, "I am so proud of my babies. You all worked very hard and deserve to spend some of your money on yourselves."

Life for us during those long hard years was a struggle but, because of my mother's prayers, love, support and unshakable faith, my siblings and I completed high school and obtained post-secondary educations. My mother is no longer with us but, we never forgot the values of prayer, hard work, family love and support that she instilled in us. To this day, when the going gets though for one of us, we still come together as a team to pull each other through.

THE UPPER CUT

Since the passing of my father, my eldest brother Jr. had steadily been grown into a young man. My mother had taken on the role of father and mother for us children. As young boys growing into manhood usually do, Jr. had become somewhat rebellious. He had started staying out late and racing fast cars. Now my mother, loving and gentle as she was, could also be a stern disciplinarian. If she told you not to do something, it was in your best interest to heed her warning. I guess without the presence of a man my brother felt that he was now the man of the house and could do as he pleased. Well he found out all too soon that was not the case. Mom had warned him on several occasions about coming in after midnight. She said we have rules in this house and one of them is no coming in after 12:00 a.m. My brother, listening to the other boys in the community, believed he was grown and didn't have to come in that early.

I had purchased a mobile home and was living next door to my mother. My brother had decided that my house would be the spot his friends would drop him off. I, being the big sister would let him come in and call my mother to say that he was with me and would probably spend the night. Well, Mom went along with that for a couple of times but, being the wise old owl that she was, she was not fooled. She stated to my brother one day, "Don't think I don't know what's going on? Believe me your mama ain't no fool. I been young once and you can't fool me".

With his usual sheepish grin on his face, my brother asked, "What are you talking about?"

"You know," said my mother, "You can act crazy if you want to but, I'm going to put my hands on you one day."

"I don't know what you talking about Mom," said my brother.

"Ok son," said my mother and walked away.

A couple of weeks passed and my brother thought that he would go out with our cousin Neal. He came to the house and said, "Aunt Leola can Jr. go with me?"

"Where y'all going?", she asked.

"Oh just up in the hills to hang out with the boys," said my cousin.

"Ok", she said. "You can go Jr. but you better be back by midnight".

"Yes ma'am", he said.

I shall never forget it. It was a hot Friday night and I was sitting on my couch watching television. I looked at the clock and it was 11:00 p.m. "Oh my goodness," I thought, "Jr. better get home on time tonight because, I think Mom is on to him coming in after his curfew and then getting out at my house."

Well sure enough midnight and no Jr. "Lord have mercy," I thought, "He is really pushing it." Little did we know that my mother had been watching through her window to see what time he would come in.

One o'clock a.m. and my cousin's car stopped in front of my house; my brother got out and walked to my front door. As soon as he put his foot on the bottom step, my mother stepped out of the shadows of the side of my mobile home and grabbed my brother by his arm.

"Where do you think you going?" she asked. "Um huh, I told you I was going to put my hands on you didn't I?" It scared my brother so much that he let out a yell.

Finally realizing that it was my mother, he replied, "Wait Mom. Wait. I couldn't help about the time because, I was riding with Neal and couldn't leave until he got ready."

"I don't want to hear it," she said. "Now get in front of me and get home."

It was really a funny sight to behold because as they walked towards her house, she was fussing and slapping the back of my brother's head. I could hear him saying, "Wait Mom, Wait. I couldn't help it."

Um huh, yea," she said. "Think you can fool me. You can't fool me boy cause I already been where you trying to go. I told you I was going to catch you."

As they disappeared out of sight, I thought to myself, "I sure wouldn't want to be him tonight."

The next day was Saturday and my mom was still upset. She told my brother to get up because the two of them needed to have a talk. Well I guess my brother had simmered over the situation during the night and decided that he was going to stand his ground. When my mother began to remind him of the house rules, he interrupted her and said, "Listen Mom, I'm the man of the house now and besides all the other boys been joking me because I have to be home at midnight and they don't".

"Well", said my mother "all the other boys don't live under my roof and I don't care what they do, but in this house you have to abide by my rules."

My brother thought that by putting some bass in his voice and raising it in protest to my mother would get him his way. My brother stomped his foot and in a loud deep voice, he said, "Well I don't think."

Bop!!! My brother never got to complete his sentence because my mother hit him with an upper cut under his chin. She hit him so hard until he fell over behind the bed. All we could see was his heels sticking up. Dazed and in a state of shock, my brother slowly climbed from behind the bed rubbing his chin.

"Child, have you lost your mind?" asked my mother. "I know so well you're not trying to bristle up at me. I don't care how grown you think you are, you will not disrespect me in my house. I am your mother and I love you but honey you better not ever try that again."

Realizing that he had gone too far, my brother embraced my mother and said, "I'm sorry Mom. I didn't mean to disrespect you. It's just that since Daddy died, I don't know what to do."

My mother soften her stance and reassured my brother that all was forgiven. She held him in her arms and told him that we were all trying to come to terms with my father's untimely and tragic death. With tears in her eyes, my mother kissed my brother and walked away.

As my mother left the room, I asked my brother, "What in the world made you think you could talk to Mom like that?"

He shook his head, rubbed his chin and said, "I don't know but, I bet you I won't try it again, cause sister Lee got a mean right hook. Man," he said, "Joe Louis ain't got nothing on her." Jr. never raised his voice at our mother again.

Although my brother felt the curfew to be unfair at the time, he now realizes that our mother was only looking out for his well being and teaching him to respect rules and guidelines.

THE FUNERAL PROCESSION

It was only three days after Christmas and the man that made the holiday so special for us was gone. Two years prior to his death, Granddaddy Van had been diagnosed with prostate cancer. The doctors felt that the cancer was in the early stage and a procedure called TURP to remove the prostate was recommended. Because of fear and a lack of an understanding of the procedure, Granddaddy refused. You have to understand that Granddaddy was a strong and proud man that had never been hospitalized nor had any major surgery and the idea of being cut was too much for him. He decided, I am an old man with grown children and grandchildren and being cut on is not an option. Life during the first two years of his diagnosis was fine but in 1985, pain and sickness began to take hold of his body. The doctors recommended chemotherapy to slow the progression of the cancer. Granddaddy was a small man and each treatment was very taxing on his frail body. The therapy would leave him very sick and weak. Finally, Granddaddy refused to take anymore chemo. He said he had made peace with his Maker, his soul was saved and was ready to go to his heavenly home. On December 28, 1985, my beloved Granddaddy Van left me.

On the day of Granddaddy's funeral, Mama Dora decided that she wanted the line up for the funeral procession to start from their home. She felt this is what he would have wanted. She said she knew that he would want to come home one last time. As the hearse followed by the family car arrived at the house, a most peculiar sight started to develop. All of the cows and horses came up to the fence beside the house and formed a straight line shoulder to shoulder. They all stood silently with their heads down as still as statues. What a sight to behold. My Mother was the first to notice and she pointed across the field and said, "Will you look at that." Everyone turned to look and was astonished at what they saw.

One of my aunts said, "I have never seen anything like that in my life! What in the world are they doing?"

My grandmother calmly said, "They are just coming to say good-bye to Van."

"What?" asked one of my cousins from Boston. "What do you mean coming to say good-bye? They couldn't possibly know what's going on, they're just animals."

"That may be," said my grandmother, "but that doesn't mean they don't know what's going on."

"Well apparently they do," said another cousin. "Just look at them standing there in total respect."

As the hearse started down the dusty dirt road from my grandparent's house, all of the animals slowly lifted their heads. The cows begin to moo, the horses began to throw their heads from side to side making whinnying noises and pawing in the sand, Granddaddy's coon hounds began to howl and the rooster gave a haunting crow. What a sad, eerie and amazing sight. It was as if the animals were mourning for the loss of their master. I guess it was only natural for the animals to react in this way because every animal on our farm was given a name by him and each animal knew its name when he called or gave them a command. He was truly a man that nurtured and cherished every blessing that God had given him. He took care of his animals just like he took care of his family. I will always remember that day, January 4, 1986, a cold Saturday afternoon when the animals came to say good-by to Granddaddy.

My siblings and I often laugh and talk about all of the special things Granddaddy use to do with us. Some of our fondest memories are of him taking us fishing on Saturdays, telling us Brer Rabbit stories around the fireplace at night and giving us slices of watermelon that he had cut with his all purpose pocket knife. We often marvel at the fact that we never saw him wash the thing. He would simply wipe the blade on his dusty overalls, close it and then put it in his pocket. He insisted that we get an education and constantly instructed us to be the best at whatever we decided to do in life.

CLOSING THOUGHTS

Every night as I lay upon my bed, I look back over my childhood with a smile. I remember my beloved mother wrapping us in blankets, telling us to run and jump into bed, tucking us in and never failing to say "Mama loves you babies"; My jovial father playing his harmonica and doing the twist as he tells us to come and dance with him; my affectionate Granddaddy Van sticking us on our cheeks with his stubby beard; my sweet Grandma Dora with outstretched arms saying come here and give mama a kiss; the fragrance from my kind Grandmother Ida's beautiful water Lillis and watching her sit on the pond bank waiting for the fish to bite; eating sweet peaches from Mama Alice's orchard and my Grandfather Israel's hearty laughter while grinding corn and emerging from the grist mill covered in white meal dust looking like a snow man.

I can still see my sister, my brothers and my cousins walking each other "piece-a-way" home and running down the dusty dirt roads laughing without a care in the world. I can still see the fields of cotton white as snow and tall stalks of corn as far as the eye can see. And, I can still see the little wooden two room Bethel Hill School with the pot bellied heater. While pondering on these things, I asked myself "Where did the time go?" As an adult, I now realize that I had a wonderful childhood that was filled with lots of love, some sorrow, some pain and yes some hard times, but I wouldn't trade it for the world, because all of the people and the events in my life that took place in the wonderful little rural community, "The Moore Place" helped shape my siblings and me into the people that we are today.

Although I no longer live in The Moore Place, I still have the opportunity to go back and visit our little wooden house, pick wildflowers, plums and pecans, stroll through the pastures and walk the roads of my childhood. The school, the store, the grist and syrup mills are no longer there, but the property that they stood on is there. Although my parents and my grandparents are no longer there, the legacy that they created for us is still there. The landscape may have changed but the morals, values, work ethics and most of all family love in our community remains intact. So, I close my story by giving thanks to GOD for Papa Tom's vision. I thank Him for my family; sometimes flawed but nevertheless my family. And, I thank Him for the good times and the bad times because, I now realize that without experiencing these things, I would not be able to witness to the world about His goodness nor share the fascinating things that happened in that *"Remnant of A Time Gone By"*, The Moore Place Community.

Romans 8:28 states "And we know that all things work together for good to them that love God, to them who are the called according to his purpose." Looking back at my family's history, all of the things we endured and what was accomplished, I can truly witness to that scripture.

Made in the USA
Columbia, SC
16 September 2024